D0232386

**Alan Titchmarsh**
**how to garden**

# Growing Fruit

**BOOKS**

FALKIRK COUNCIL LIBRARIES

634     BN

Published in 2010 by BBC Books, an imprint of
Ebury Publishing, a Random House Group Company

Copyright © Alan Titchmarsh 2010

The right of Alan Titchmarsh to be identified as the
author of this work has been asserted in accordance
with Sections 77 and 78 of the Copyright, Designs and
Patents Act 1988.

All rights reserved. No part of this publication may be
reproduced, stored in a retrieval system, or transmitted
in any form or by any means, electronic, mechanical,
photocopying, recording or otherwise, without the
prior permission of the copyright owner.

The Random House Group Limited Reg. No. 954009

Addresses for companies within the Random House
Group can be found at
**www.randomhouse.co.uk**

The Random House Group Limited supports The Forest
Stewardship Council (FSC), the leading international
forest certification organisation. All our titles that are
printed on Greenpeace approved FSC certified paper
carry the FSC logo. Our paper procurement policy can
be found at www.rbooks.co.uk/environment

A CIP catalogue record for this book is available from
the British Library.

ISBN 978 1 84 607 4011

Produced by OutHouse!
Shalbourne, Marlborough, Wiltshire SN8 3QJ

BBC BOOKS
COMMISSIONING EDITOR: Lorna Russell
PROJECT EDITOR: Caroline McArthur
PRODUCTION: Bridget Fish

OUTHOUSE!
CONCEPT DEVELOPMENT & SERIES DESIGN:
 Elizabeth Mallard-Shaw, Sharon Cluett
PROJECT MANAGEMENT: Polly Boyd
ART DIRECTOR: Robin Whitecross
CONTRIBUTING EDITOR: Jo Weeks
PROJECT EDITOR: Polly Boyd
DESIGNER: Sharon Cluett
ILLUSTRATOR: Lizzie Harper

PHOTOGRAPHS by Jonathan Buckley except where
credited otherwise on page 128

Colour origination by Altaimage, London
Printed and bound by Firmengruppe APPL,
Wemding, Germany

# Contents

# Introduction

Gardening is one of the best and most fulfilling activities on earth, but it can sometimes seem complicated and confusing. The answers to problems can usually be found in books, but big fat gardening books can be rather daunting. Where do you start? How can you find just the information you want without wading through lots of stuff that is not appropriate to your particular problem? Well, a good index is helpful, but sometimes a smaller book devoted to one particular subject fits the bill better – especially if it is reasonably priced and if you have a small garden where you might not be able to fit in everything suggested in a larger volume.

The *How to Garden* books aim to fill that gap – even if sometimes it may be only a small one. They are clearly set out and written, I hope, in a straightforward, easy-to-understand style. I don't see any point in making gardening complicated, when much of it is based on common sense and observation. (All the key techniques are explained and illustrated, and I've included plenty of tips and tricks of the trade.)

There are suggestions on the best plants and the best varieties to grow in particular situations and for a particular effect. I've tried to keep the information crisp and to the point so that you can find what you need quickly and easily and then put your new-found knowledge into practice. Don't worry if you're not familiar with the Latin names of plants. They are there to make sure you can find the plant as it will be labelled in the nursery or garden centre, but where appropriate I have included common names, too. Forgetting a plant's name need not stand in your way when it comes to being able to grow it.

Above all, the *How to Garden* books are designed to fill you with passion and enthusiasm for your garden and all that its creation and care entails, from designing and planting it to maintaining it and enjoying it. For more than fifty years gardening has been my passion, and that initial enthusiasm for watching plants grow, for trying something new and for just being outside pottering has never faded. If anything I am keener on gardening now than I ever was and get more satisfaction from my plants every day. It's not that I am simply a romantic, but rather that I have learned to look for the good in gardens and in plants, and there is lots to be found. Oh, there are times when I fail – when my plants don't grow as well as they should and I need to try harder. But where would I rather be on a sunny day? Nowhere!

The *How to Garden* handbooks will, I hope, allow some of that enthusiasm – childish though it may be – to rub off on you, and the information they contain will, I hope, make you a better gardener, as well as opening your eyes to the magic of plants and flowers.

# Becoming a fruit grower

Almost any garden space is suitable for growing fruit. Of course, a dedicated fruit garden is ideal, but the tiniest outdoor plot can fit in a few strawberry plants – they'll even grow in a hanging basket – and there are plenty of other fruits that will grow in a restricted space, including apples, pears and cherries. In most cases you can enjoy your own home-grown fruit the year after it's planted.

# Why grow your own?

While many people are quite happy to consider growing vegetables, the idea of cultivating fruit can seem a bit more daunting – but it needn't be. In fact, many types of fruit are much easier to grow than vegetables – they're less prone to pests and diseases, and once they're established they need considerably less attention, with work being weekly or monthly rather than daily. In fact, there are almost as many reasons for growing fruit as there are fruit varieties.

## Taste and freshness

Shops simply can't compete with home-grown produce when it comes to freshness, ripeness and flavour. Think of those rock hard plums, apricots, peaches and nectarines at your supermarket. They had to be picked before they were ripe so they would travel well, and as a result their taste suffers. You might get only a dozen or so apricots or peaches off your own tree, but you can pick them when they're at the peak of perfection, warmed by the sun and literally oozing juice and flavour. If you grow plums, you'll have more than you know what to do with most years.

## Something different

Take a walk along a supermarket fruit aisle and you'll always see apples, oranges and bananas. Nowadays, you'll also see strawberries, blueberries and raspberries almost every month of the year. But how often do you see blackcurrants, whitecurrants and redcurrants? What about rhubarb and gooseberries? If

you happen to like these rather unfashionable fruit, you're often out of luck when searching for them in the shops. And if you do manage to find them, they may be bruised and

unattractive because they don't really take kindly to travelling.

Depending on the amount of space you have available, you can grow as many plants as you have an appetite for, and you can try a range of different varieties – not just the ones that travel well and keep for a long time, which is what commercial growers tend to concentrate on. And finally, a very good reason for growing your own is that the fruit won't have done stellar mileage to get to your table, which has to be good for our overburdened planet.

It's so satisfying to wander through your fruit garden gathering produce that you've seen develop from flowers through to fruit. Redcurrants are well worth growing, as you so rarely find them fresh in the shops.

### Don't forget

Many fruit trees are attractive decorative plants that enhance the garden with their leaves, flowers and fruit, even if you have no plans to eat their produce.

# Deciding what to grow

Once you've made up your mind to include fruit in your garden or allotment, you have the fun of choosing what to grow. It goes without saying that you'll want to include fruit that you and your family like, but beyond that there are quite a few factors you need to take into account to ensure your foray into fruit growing is as successful as possible.

Almost every garden has the space to accommodate at least one apple tree, and the traditional cooker 'Bramley's Seedling' is an excellent choice, particularly if you like apple crumbles and pies. It is also incredibly easy to grow, needing little care.

## Your plot

The size of your garden is a major consideration, and it's important to tailor your ambitions to the space you have available. That said, it's possible to fit almost all commonly grown fruits into even quite a small plot, as long as you don't expect to become self-sufficient in them. (For details on growing fruit in a small garden, *see* pages 20–1).

The vast majority of fruit needs a sunny, sheltered site and prefers a fertile, well-drained soil. There are ways of improving your soil to make it more suitable (*see* pages 26–7), but if you live on the windy top of a hillside, you need to consider creating shelter. You can also choose fruit that copes more easily with difficult conditions, as far as both soil and aspect are concerned (*see* Challenging conditions box, page 19). Lack of sun is more difficult to remedy, especially where it is trees or buildings outside your own garden creating the shade, although some fruit will tolerate a little shade.

## Your location

One of the aims of modern plant breeding has been to obtain more reliable crops in a wider range of growing conditions. This has vastly increased the number of fruit varieties available to gardeners, and as a result most fruit can be grown in

### Don't forget

Most types of fruit need plenty of sun, but soft fruit such as blackberries, raspberries, gooseberries and strawberries will tolerate dappled shade for part of the day. However, the flavour of sun-grown fruit is always better.

most places nowadays. However, there are certain instances where your location must be taken into account, otherwise you'll be in for a lot of disappointment. Apricots, for example, are happier in southern and central parts of Britain and usually struggle outdoors in northern Britain and Wales, where they are better in a greenhouse. Similarly, peaches tend to do well in eastern England, such as in East Anglia, but are much more difficult to grow in the Midlands and further north. Figs, melons and grapes may produce crops, but in many areas they require plenty of input for very little output. If you're really keen, they're worth a go, but you will need to work quite hard to achieve success. The A–Z of fruit (*see* pages 74–115) will give you all the information you need, so check there before making your purchases.

## Your energy levels

Fruit growing is not such hard work as vegetable growing, but the plants do need attention from time to

Melons are challenging as they need plenty of care, and even then they are difficult to grow well, especially outdoors and in poor summers. However, if you do succeed, you'll never forget the taste of your own home-grown fruit.

time. For instance, strawberries put out stems (runners) in summer, with new plants on the ends and middles. These need to be removed or rooted (*see* pages 114–15), otherwise your strawberry patch or pot will end up a tangled mess of stems and leaves with precious little fruit, and what there is will be difficult to find.

All fruit trees need regular assessment for pruning, and those that are being trained as cordons, espaliers, stepovers or fans (*see* pages

13–14, 64–8) need more regular pruning than those that are being allowed to develop more naturally (*see* page 13). Vines, particularly grapes, will need firm treatment and keeping within bounds if they're to be fully productive (*see* pages 17, 71–2). Then there are weeds to root out and feeding to be done, as well as other jobs that ensure your plants are healthy and happy. After rhubarb, which is satisfied with a yearly dollop of well-rotted compost or manure, blueberries and cranberries are among the least demanding fruit. Natural-shaped bush fruits are not hard work either, but even they need some pruning and tidying up. If you're unsure of how much time you'll be able to devote to your fruit, start with just a couple of plants and expand your collection as and when you feel like it.

An espalier pear makes an attractive feature against a fence or wall, where conditions will favour the production of plenty of flowers, and hence fruit. Espaliers need regular pruning but the effort will be more than repaid.

# Ways of growing tree fruit

Before you make a final decision about what to grow, it's helpful to look at the different ways in which you can grow fruit, taking into account the space you have available, the amount of time you have for pruning and the look you want to create. Although fruit naturally grows on trees and bushes, and along vines and canes (*see* pages 16–17), fruit growers have come up with a variety of other ingenious ways of training these plants so that they can perform well in a range of garden situations.

If left to their own devices, most fruit trees eventually grow tall and wide, making them hard to accommodate in the average garden and their produce difficult to harvest. However, for centuries gardeners have been looking for ways of making plants smaller. In the case of fruit, this is done using two principal methods: by raising fruit on rootstocks that won't allow them to grow too big (*see* page 15); and by training them through pruning to

stay small (*see* pages 54–73). The training work is usually carried out by the gardener, but in the case of rootstocks the trees are already grafted before you buy them, so when choosing apples, apricots, cherries, peaches, nectarines, pears and plums you'll need to bear the type of rootstock in mind.

In fruit growing there are two basic types of tree: freestanding and supported, and within those two basic types are a number of variations.

## Types of fruit

As far as the gardener is concerned there are two main types of fruit plants: tree fruit (also known as top fruit) and soft fruit, and these are further subdivided into groups. These give some indication of fruit type, cultivation requirements and, of course, growth habit.

**TREE FRUIT**
**Pome** Apple, pear
**Stone** Apricot, cherry, nectarine, peach, plum
**Nut** Almond, hazelnut, sweet chestnut, walnut
**Other** Fig, mulberry, quince

**SOFT FRUIT**
**Bedding** Rhubarb, strawberry
**Bush** Blackcurrant, redcurrant, whitecurrant, gooseberry, jostaberry, blueberry, cranberry
**Cane** Raspberry, blackberry, loganberry, and many hybrids of raspberries or blackberries, such as tayberry, loganberry, tummelberry
**Vine** Grape, kiwi, melon, passionfruit

Nowadays, bush-form fruit trees are probably the most popular trees for gardens and orchards: they're compact and neat, as well as being relatively easy to prune and harvest fruit from.

Pears, apples and plums all make good dwarf pyramids. These are a bit trickier to prune than the bush type but are taller and more elegant.

Standards and half-standards are defined by the length of bare trunk below their branches. Both look wonderful as specimen trees, but standards need plenty of space.

## Freestanding trees

These trees can be grown without support after the first couple of years. Their final height depends on the rootstock and the variety. They require some pruning to keep their shape and productivity. Bush-form trees, pyramids and columns are all suitable for growing in containers. (For details on how to prune freestanding trees, *see* pages 58–61.)

### Bush form
This has a bushy network of branches above a trunk that is 45–75cm (18–30in) high. The smallest bush trees are the very dwarf apples at 2m (6ft).
■ Candidates: Apples, apricots, cherries, figs, pears, peaches, nectarines, plums, cobnuts, filberts.

### Pyramid
This is like a bush, except the trunk is taller and the branches are pruned to produce a conical shape. Pyramids can be as small as 2.2m (7ft) high and 1.2m (4ft) wide.
■ Candidates: Apples, cherries, pears, plums.

### Standard and half-standard
These are usually grown in larger gardens and commercial orchards, as they grow quite tall. The trunks of standards are about 2m (6ft) and half-standards 1.2m (4ft).
■ Candidates: Apples, cherries, pears, plums.

### Columnar
With a slender trunk and very short branches, a columnar tree is bought ready trained (usually tagged as a ballerina or pillarette/ minarette) and grows to 2.5m (8ft).
■ Candidates: Apples, cherries, mulberries, pears, plums.

### Free-form
Several fruit trees are freestanding and are allowed to grow into their natural shape.
■ Candidates: Mulberries, quinces, almonds, sweet chestnuts, walnuts, hazels (though these can be coppiced if necessary).

## Supported trees

Supported trees are grown on a framework of wires, either stretched between posts or attached to a wall or fence. They can be very decorative but do require a lot of work (pruning at least twice a year to maintain their shape) and tend to be shorter-lived and less productive than freestanding trees. A big advantage is that they enable you to grow fruit in a tiny area. (For details on how to prune supported trees, *see* pages 64–8.)

### Cordon
A cordon usually has a single main stem. This is most often

Apples are among the most versatile fruit trees, lending themselves to being grown in all sorts of ways. Here, a row of cordon apples makes an appealing hedge.

Apricots, peaches, nectarines and plums are all worth trying as fans. They're usually trained against a wall or fence and benefit from the additional shelter.

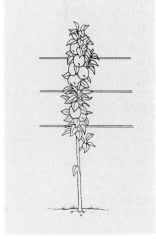

Cordons make narrow trees that can be trained vertically or at an angle to make the most of a small space.

grown at a 45-degree angle, when it may be referred to as an oblique cordon, but cordons are also suitable for growing vertically. A variation on a vertical cordon is to have two main stems, which is more common in soft fruit (see page 17). Cordons are normally grown on a dwarf rootstock (see opposite). The branches may be encouraged from low down on the trunk, about 45cm (18in) above the ground, or higher up, depending on the desired effect.

■ Candidates: Apples, pears, plums, redcurrants, whitecurrants.

Espalier  Like a cordon, an espalier has a single main stem, but this is grown upright. Opposite pairs of branches growing off it are tied horizontally to wires to produce a neat, symmetrical shape; this is difficult to achieve, so it's best to buy ready-trained espaliers. The branches are allowed to grow longer than on cordons, so espaliers take up more space but tend to be more attractive than cordons.

■ Candidates: Apples, pears.

Fan-trained  This is a bit like an espalier, in that the tree is grown flat against its support and the branches are tied in to a system of supports. However, a fan is more informal: the main stem branches are much lower and can grow more upright, and the sideshoots are allowed to grow longer and with less shaping. Fans are usually trained against walls or fences and are ideal for fruit trees that need shelter and warmth.

■ Candidates: Almonds, apples, apricots, cherries, figs, peaches, nectarines, pears, plums.

Stepover  This is a single-tiered espalier, trained at a very low height (30cm/12in), so you can literally step over it, as its name suggests. It makes a useful edging plant (see page 21).

■ Candidates: Apples on a very dwarf rootstock (see opposite).

Spindlebush  This is rarely found in gardens. It's a variation on the freestanding pyramid. The trunk is supported by a stake and all the branches are tied down to keep them horizontal, to break apical dominance (see box, page 61).

■ Candidates: Apples, pears.

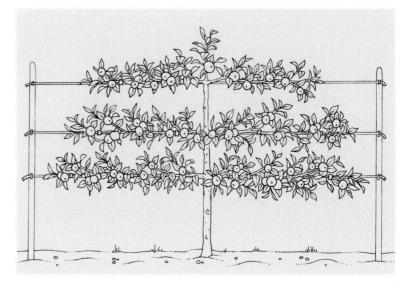

Espaliers are an elegant way of growing trees in a confined area while still getting plenty of fruit. They can be used to create a hedge around a vegetable garden or to divide an ornamental garden.

It might seem that stepovers are nothing but a curiosity, but when looked after well, these tiny trees can produce a reasonable crop.

Most fruit trees are grown on roots that are not their own. These roots are called rootstocks and there are a few good reasons for their use. Rootstocks are used to impose certain characteristics on the trees, such as height, vigour or the ability to grow in particular conditions. They also enable the trees to fruit at a younger age than they might do naturally.

Although the traditional apple tree on its own roots makes a beautiful centrepiece in a large garden (above), newer varieties on specially selected rootstocks offer modern gardeners more scope (left).

As you will know, fruit varieties are distinguished by names such as 'Cox's Orange Pippin' apple or 'Comice' pear; these named varieties don't grow 'true' from their seed. That means if you planted, say, the seed of a 'Cox's Orange Pippin', you wouldn't get a 'Cox's Orange Pippin' tree. Grafting shoots or even just buds of these varieties onto specially raised rootstocks is the only way to propagate them.

### Fruit tree rootstocks

Apples have six main rootstocks. For most gardens M27, M9 and M26 are the ones to choose. M27 is very dwarfing, M9 is a little bigger; both these need good growing conditions and permanent support. M26 is semi-dwarfing and will need support for a couple of years if it is grown as a freestanding tree, but it is also recommended for growing cordons and dwarf pyramids (*see* pages 12–14).

Cherries are mostly grown on Colt rootstocks, which grow to about 5m (16ft). Gisela 5 is a more recently introduced, highly productive semi-dwarf rootstock.

Pears have three rootstocks: Quince A, Quince C and BA29. Quince A copes with poorish soils, Quince C is better on more fertile soils and will give earlier fruit, while BA29 is a little taller and more vigorous than Quince A, but is good on dry soils.

Plums have six rootstocks: St Julien A, Pixy, Ferlenain, Myrobalan B, Mussel and Brompton. St Julien A is a compact all-rounder that can cope with poorish soil; Pixy and Ferlenain are also small but need good soil. Mussel is quite compact, but can produce suckers and so is not recommended. Myrobalan B and Brompton are vigorous, so best avoided in smaller gardens.

Apricots are raised on Pixy, Torinel and St Julien A, while peaches and nectarines are grown on the plum rootstock Pixy.

M27

M9, Gisela 5, Torinel, M26

Pixy, Ferlenain, Quince C

Colt, St Julien A, Quince A, BA29

The eventual size of any tree grown on a particular rootstock will vary depending on growing conditions and the sort of pruning regime it undergoes. However, this illustration gives a good idea of the relative sizes achieved by the various rootstocks three to five years after planting and their possible size at maturity.

# Ways of growing soft fruit and vine fruit

The types of fruit that are known as 'soft' are a more variable bunch than tree fruit in both growth habit and cultivation requirements. The smallest are bedding fruit, which are compact and reasonably tidy in habit, while the largest are the vines and the cane fruit, which need careful control if they're not to make a nuisance of themselves. Somewhere in the middle are the bush fruit, which are moderately well behaved, although they do need some pruning to give their best.

## Bedding fruit

Strawberries and rhubarb are the two bedding fruits most often found in our gardens. Strawberries can be grown in the ground in a fruit garden or in containers of every conceivable design, from hanging containers (*see* page 20) to tiered tubs (*see* page 33). Rhubarb makes a long-lived foliage plant and is easily kept under control in a fruit garden, but it can reach 2m (6ft) across.

## Bush fruit

Although they may look quite similar, the various bush fruit are grown in quite different ways.

**Multi-stemmed** This is where the shrub either naturally produces several stems, or is encouraged to produce multiple stems by planting about 5cm (2in) or more below the depth it was in the pot.
- Candidates: Blackcurrants, blueberries, cranberries.

**Leg** The bushy shape is created above a single bare stem about 15cm (6in) tall. Branches that start to grow on this length of stem are removed back to their base.
- Candidates: Gooseberries, redcurrants, whitecurrants.

**Standard** The bush fruit has been grafted onto the rootstock and stem of a more vigorous variety, resulting in a long, bare stem up to 1m (3ft) tall, with bushy growth at the top.
- Candidate: Gooseberries.

Growing strawberries in containers is a good way of ensuring you don't have to share your crop with slugs and snails, and it reduces the chances of the fruit rotting on the damp ground of a bed or border.

For a crossover between functional and decorative, there is little to beat this double-cordon redcurrant. Once the two main stems are established, double cordons are trained in the same way as single cordons.

Long ago it was found that the most productive way to grow grapes was by the double Guyot system. This will appeal to neat and tidy gardeners, but you can also get a reasonable crop with a more relaxed approach, for example by growing them on a pergola (*see* pages 71–2).

Where space is plentiful, passionfruit can be left to do their own thing. They often become a tangled mass of stems and leaves, but this won't stop them from producing fruit.

**Cordon**  Bush fruit cordons are similar to tree fruit cordons (*see* pages 13–14), but the main stem is usually upright.
- Candidates: Gooseberries, redcurrants, whitecurrants.

**Fan**  These are similar to tree fruit fans (*see* pages 13–14) but not as big.
- Candidates: Gooseberries, redcurrants, whitecurrants.

## Cane fruit

As far as cultivation is concerned, there are two key ways of growing cane fruit: upright and horizontally. Both need a strong system of supporting wires, which can be set up in the open garden or against a wall or fence.

**Upright**  Raspberries are grown vertically, tied in formally to their canes to produce a hedge-like arrangement of stems. Blackberries and their hybrids can also be grown vertically and informally, on arches and other decorative supports.

**Horizontally**  Blackberries and their hybrids can be woven around wires or tied in to produce a fan.

## Vine fruit

As the name implies, vine fruit grow on climbing or scrambling plants. These are mostly very vigorous and must be kept strictly within bounds, otherwise they become very untidy and produce masses of greenery and growth at the expense of the fruit. They can be quite attractive.

**Espalier**  This is similar to a fruit tree espalier (*see* page 14).
- Candidate: Kiwi fruit.

**Cordon**  This is similar to a fruit tree cordon (*see* pages 13–14), except that the main stem can be grown vertically or horizontally, or both – for example, vertically up the post of a pergola and horizontally along the pergola joists. Vine cordons may also have two main stems.
- Candidate: Grapes.

**Double Guyot**  This is the way most grapes are grown outdoors, including all those acres of grapes grown for wine all over the world. The vine is grown on a single trunk or leg at the top of which each year two shoots (rods) are trained horizontally, and from both of these three vertical stems are allowed to grow (*see* page 94). The appearance is not as beautiful as a cordon vine grown over a pergola but the fruit production is much better.

**Informal**  Melons and passionfruit are often allowed to grow naturally with their stems being tied in or woven around supports as needed.

# Planning your fruit garden

By now you're armed with all the information you need to plan your fruit garden. If you're going to devote a particular area to fruit, it pays to think carefully about how you site your plants within it. Most fruit-producing plants remain in one place for their whole life, so you want to put them in the best possible position to begin with. In fact, the same goes for plants that are going to be integrated into the garden.

your plants get off to a good start and continue to benefit throughout their lives. You can group together plants that need similar growing conditions and you can also plant pollinating partners (see box, opposite) near each other to improve your chances of getting a good crop.

## A dedicated fruit garden

The plus side of having a dedicated fruit garden is that it's simpler to create shelter for the whole area if necessary, and easier to provide protection from birds, too, in the

form of a fruit cage for example. In addition, if you're starting from scratch, you can dig over the area or at least part of it, remove weeds and incorporate plenty of well-rotted compost (see pages 26–7), to ensure

## Planning and choosing fruit

To begin plotting your fruit garden, you need to know the eventual height and width of each of your chosen plants and their preferred spacings. This information is given

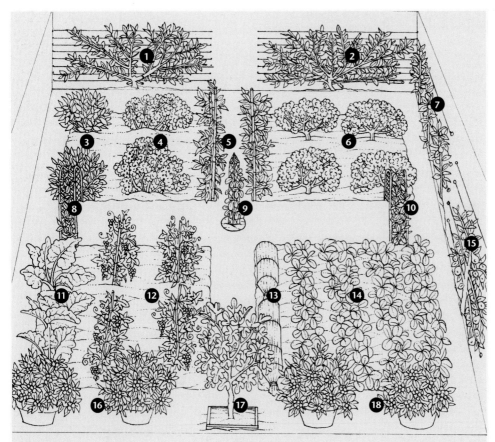

With careful planning, it's amazing what can be fitted into a small space. This simple plan shows a fruit garden that is 10m (33ft) square.

1 Fan apricot
2 Fan cherry
3 Jostaberries
4 Blackcurrants
5 Raspberries
6 Gooseberries
7 Cordon apples
8 Blackberries
9 Kiwi fruit
10 Tayberries
11 Rhubarb
12 Grapes
13 Melons
14 Strawberries
15 Espalier pear
16 Blueberries
17 Fig
18 Blueberries

For flowers to produce fruit, pollination must take place. Luckily, the majority of fruit plants are self-fertile, which means that the flowers can pollinate themselves or other flowers on the same plant. However, there are some very important exceptions where the plant must have pollen from another variety of the same fruit in order to produce a crop.

In suburban areas, it's likely that a garden near you will have a pollinating partner for whatever you choose, but it would be a terrible disappointment if it didn't, as you simply wouldn't get any fruit. So, when you buy apples, pears, plums, cherries and kiwi fruits, you need to check whether the variety you choose requires a pollinating partner; some are self-fertile. The people who raise fruit plants for sale know that this is a bit complicated for the average gardener, so the label should tell you all you need to know. (The A–Z directory also indicates where pollinating partners are needed and which plants are suitable, *see* pages 74–115.)

for the recommended plants in the A–Z of fruit directory (*see* pages 74–115) and you should also be able to get it from the label on the plants you buy. However, it's worth doing the planning before you make your purchases, so be prepared to spend a little time at the nursery or garden centre doing some research beforehand. This also gives you the opportunity to discuss your requirements with staff, who should be able to advise you on the best varieties for your area (*see* pages 10–11), and to see what's available, as well as order anything you fancy.

If you've got the space for a number of plants, it is easy to plan for a succession of fruit, as many varieties ripen at slightly different times. For example, it's possible to pick apples straight off the trees from late summer into early winter without having to think about storage. And if you have storage facilities, you can go on enjoying them until late spring the following year.

## Planting in the right place

It's important to position taller plants, such as larger fruit trees and nuts, somewhere where they won't cast too much shade on smaller plants. Next come the larger vines and canes, then the bush fruits, and finally the strawberries and rhubarb. If you plan to erect a fruit cage, these can all be housed within it, although the rhubarb needs no such protection. Tender fruit, such as figs, peaches and melons, need to be grown beside a sheltered sunny wall or fence or in a greenhouse. Fit in more plants by lining paths with stepovers or espaliers and clothing arches and fences with vines and cane fruit.

Fruit does best in easy growing conditions with plenty of water, shelter and fertile soil. However, it's possible to have fruit in less than perfect situations, although you may not get as much and you may have to work a bit harder for what you do get.

### COLD AND WINDY SITES

Cold and windy sites are very difficult for fruit, because the flowers need pollination and pollinating insects are discouraged by wind. Cold winds when the flowers appear can result in frost damage too. Choose low-growing fruit, such as cranberries, blueberries and strawberries, and provide protection (*see* pages 46–7) during cold and windy spells. Hazels, cobnuts and blackberries will succeed on windy sites, although they're happier with some shelter.

### DRY AND HOT SPOTS

These are much less of a problem as long as you water well, and that means really well and on a regular basis. Plants such as figs, apricots, citrus fruit, peaches, grapes, passionfruit and melons really need heat to do well, so choose these, but bear in mind that they're also prone to damage by cold, so protect them if cold weather is forecast.

### CHALKY SOIL

Chalky soil is generally considered unsuitable for fruit, although you might succeed with just a few plants to which you can give plenty of tender loving care. If you garden on chalk, choose fruit that will grow in containers (*see* pages 20 and 32–5), or consider constructing one or two large raised beds, which you can fill with more suitable soil.

### DAMP SOIL

Very damp soil should be improved with the addition of plenty of organic matter and grit (*see* page 27) before you attempt to grow fruit, unless you're trying to grow cranberries or blueberries, both of which really like these conditions, just as long as the soil is acidic. To grow a wider range of fruit, you'll need to improve drainage or make raised beds.

If you'd rather not have a formal fruit garden, it's very easy to slot fruit (here, a plum) into your ornamental beds, where they'll look decorative and produce a good crop too.

There is absolutely no reason why a small garden cannot be home to a wide range of fruit, both tree fruit and soft fruit. By choosing your varieties carefully, and pruning and training on a regular basis, you'll be able to grow a selection of your favourite fruit very successfully, as well as having an attractive display of flowers and produce for many months of the year.

Some types of fruit are naturally small, some have smallness bred into them and others can be kept small through pruning. All of the fruits shown here are possible candidates for a small garden. ① Blackberry 'Oregon Thornless'. ② Gooseberry 'Whinham's Industry'. ③ Blueberry 'Ivanhoe'.

## Growing in pots

Surprisingly, perhaps, pots make a very good place to grow fruit, as long as you provide the plants with what they need (see pages 32–5). The first choice for containers has to be strawberries, which can be grown just about anywhere. They can be very productive in special pots with several extra holes around the sides that allow for additional plants (see page 33), and in hanging baskets, which also have the benefit of keeping them out of the way of other interested parties, such as slugs. Melons are also excellent in large containers on a sheltered, sunny patio.

Bush fruit such as gooseberries, blackcurrants, cranberries and blueberries can be kept quite small and make good candidates for pots. This makes it easier to protect them from birds, too, as you can throw nets over them individually when the fruit ripens, although the netting will be a bit unsightly. Blueberries and cranberries are very particular about soil and water (see pages 84 and 88), so growing them in pots can be a positive advantage, as you can provide them with exactly the conditions they like.

Fruit trees on dwarf rootstocks (see page 15) or the columnar, pillarette/ minarette or ballerina type (see opposite) are perfect for pots and can be used to create attractive focal points on the patio, as can figs and citrus fruit. In fact, figs are often better with their roots restricted, which is what happens in a pot, and containers are essential for growing citrus fruit in Britain, since they must be brought indoors for the winter. Choose large tubs and pots and be sure to attend very carefully to feeding and watering. Larger trees and bushes must be sheltered from strong winds, which cause damage and might blow them over.

Make the best use of all available space by hanging containers on frames and from walls or fences. Here, colanders make stylish and practical containers for strawberries.

## Along walls and fences

Having read Ways of growing tree fruit (pages 12–14), you'll know that you can grow fruit trees on walls and along wires in very restricted spaces, as espaliers, cordons, fans and stepovers. Apples, apricots, cherries, figs, pears, peaches, plums and nectarines are all within your grasp this way. Gooseberries, redcurrants and whitecurrants can be trained as cordons or fans too. Although such highly trained, supported fruit takes quite a lot of work to maintain, it is also productive for its size, so the input is balanced by the output.

Cane fruits such as blackberries and their hybrids are also suitable for growing against a wall or fence, in fact this is often the best spot for them as it makes curtailing their excessive behaviour much more straightforward. You can get thornless varieties too – essential in a small space. The best place for passionfruit is also against a wall or fence, where their beautiful flowers can be appreciated and where they get the shelter and warmth they need to produce fruit.

## Up arches and pergolas

Vines such as grapes and kiwis can scramble around fences and walls, and above your head on arches and along pergolas. If you have this type of space available, you can consider them in the smallest garden. Again, they're very attractive as garden plants: kiwis produce pretty flowers and grapes have good autumn colour.

Blackberries and their hybrids make good candidates for an arch or trellis, as long as you tie them in regularly; remember to choose the thornless varieties. Raspberries can be grown in a restricted space but they do best when they're trained on purpose-built supports. They look good along a path beside the vegetable garden, for example, but a bit too formal in most flower gardens.

Apples can grow very well in containers as long as they're watered well and in a sheltered spot so the wind won't blow them over. Here, ballerina apples 'Polka' and 'Rajka' make an attractive pair in matching pots and have plenty of fruit.

Stepovers make an excellent edging for vegetable beds and are very productive for their size. With their sculptural branches all knotted and twisted, they're as attractive bare in winter as they are fully dressed in summer.

The pale flowers of this fan-trained morello cherry look wonderful against the red brick wall. Later, reflected heat from the wall will help ripen the fruit. Fan-training is a good way of making use of vertical features in small gardens.

# Planting and growing

Once you've decided what to include in your fruit garden, you can start to prepare the site and plant it up. If you're using an area that is already cultivated, your job will be much easier, but it's still worth spending a bit of time making sure it's weed-free and that the soil is in good condition. If you're starting from scratch, you've got a bit of work to do before you can begin planting.

# Tools and equipment

As with any sort of gardening, it's important to have the right tools to do the job. There are few tools specifically needed for fruit growing, so if you already have any sort of garden, you're likely to have most of those you'll need, the main ones being a spade and a fork. For specific pruning tools, *see* page 56.

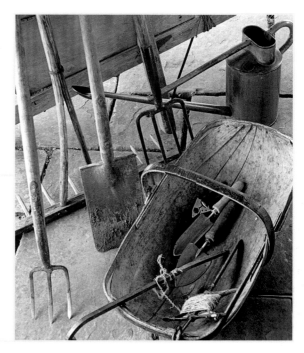

## Digging, planting and weeding

For digging, turning the soil and planting, you'll need a spade and a fork. Forks are excellent at loosening clumps of soil and extricating stones and troublesome weeds. Spades are good for digging light soils and making planting holes. Use a spade for manoeuvring compost and manure into a wheelbarrow and onto planting areas, and a fork to incorporate them into the soil.

Draw or chop hoes are ideal for weeding between soft fruit bushes and around raspberries, grapes and so on, particularly if you have a traditional fruit garden with the plants in rows. Their blade is at a right angle to a longish shaft and they're used in a chopping motion

Most of us start off with a few basic tools and acquire more as the years go by. But it's very often the old stalwarts, such as spades, forks and hand trowels, that get the most use.

to cut down the weeds. Alternatively, use a push or Dutch hoe, which has a very slightly angled blade at the end of a long shaft. You slide the blade just under the soil surface, and it slices through weeds as it goes.

Choose a good-quality hoe with a sharp blade, otherwise it will uproot rather than decapitate, and uprooted weeds can easily reroot.

A rake with short parallel teeth comes in handy for levelling the soil in preparation for planting. Pick one that has a bit of weight in the head, otherwise it will simply bounce over the soil.

## Smaller jobs

A hand fork and trowel are useful for planting and weeding around strawberries. They're also good for grubbing out deep-rooted weeds and keeping the earth around the stems

of newly planted bushes and trees weed-free. Choose a trowel with a shaped blade (not too shallow) that has sharp edges, and a fork with strong tines. Both fork and trowel should have comfortable handles.

Garden knives are useful for various trimming jobs, and secateurs for pruning and thinning are a must.

You'll also need some equipment to protect your plants: for fruit trees, you'll need a selection of stakes and tree ties to prevent wind rock from damaging the tree. If you have a rabbit or deer population nearby, you should consider tree guards.

For watering and liquid feeding, you'll need a watering can and, preferably, a water butt, as well as the feed itself (*see* pages 38–9).

Finally, a wheelbarrow is very useful for transporting soil, manure and plants around the garden.

### Shredders

If you have a fruit garden, it's well worth investing in a shredder to take care of your prunings. Woody material takes years to compost down unless it's shredded, after which it can be added in moderate amounts to the compost heap, or used as a mulch around your plants.

Electric shredders are relatively inexpensive and capable of shredding branches up to 4cm (1¾in) thick. Always check the capacity of the machine. Petrol-driven shredders can usually cope with thicker branches but are much more expensive to buy and often rather large for the average garden.

# Site and soil

It's important to choose the brightest, most sheltered spot possible for your fruit garden. The ideal site faces south or south west, with shelter from prevailing winds and weather, which also come from the south west. In addition, it should have protection on the eastern and northern sides, the direction of the coldest winds (*see* page 47). Fruit plants grow best in deep, fertile soil that drains freely. If you don't already know what type of soil you've got, it's well worth having a dig to find out.

## Soil texture

Garden soil consists of varying amounts of loam, sand, chalk (limestone), clay and/or peat (*see* box, opposite). It can also be stony, solid, crumbly and so on. All these characteristics have an effect on the plants growing in it and can tell you something about its likely fertility. Even if you have the most unpromising soil type, it's possible to improve it. In fact, even the best soils benefit from the addition of a bit of muck (*see* page 27).

Loam  The gardener's dream, loam is easy to dig, well drained but moisture retentive, and naturally fertile – perfect for growing fruit.

Sandy soil  Water drains out of sandy soil very quickly, taking nutrients with it as it goes, so the soil will need regular feeding.

A sunny, sheltered site will make your fruit garden a perfect spot for both the plants and the pollinating insects. You'll enjoy it there, too.

Chalky soil  This is reasonably fertile and well drained, but usually it is also shallow and alkaline, neither of which is ideal for fruit.

Peaty soil  Found in moorland environments, this is naturally low in nutrients. It absorbs moisture, but also drains quickly.

Clay soil  The individual particles that make up clay soil are very fine and stick tightly together. This means clay tends to retain moisture and nutrients, but during dry weather it bakes hard. The main disadvantage of clay soil for fruit growers is that drainage can be poor.

## Soil pH

The chemical content of soil can vary from very acid to very alkaline. The scale used to measure soil acidity or alkalinity is called pH – and it runs from pH 1 (very acid) through pH 7 (neutral) to pH 14 (very alkaline). Luckily, the extremes (1 and 14) are rare. The chemical balance of the soil can make certain nutrients unavailable to plants, so it has an impact on how well they grow. Fruit grows best on neutral to slightly acid soil.

The most effective way to find out your soil pH is to get a kit from the garden centre. You can also make some deductions by inspecting your soil – chalky soil is alkaline, peaty soil is acid. Also, look at the plants growing locally in your area. If you're surrounded by camellias or rhododendrons, you're likely to have acidic soil. Their leaves tend to go yellow in alkaline areas, as the plants lack the iron they need to grow well.

A very simple soil-testing kit can reveal much about your garden's soil. The soil in this test tube is just on the acid side of neutral, indicated by the greenish colour. There are also kits available that show soil nutrient levels.

### Don't forget

While you can slightly influence the pH of your soil by adding chemical 'remedies', such alterations are only temporary and they can be expensive, so are not really recommended. If you have very alkaline soil, the best solution is to grow fruit in containers or raised beds filled with neutral or slightly acid soil.

## Your garden soil

Whatever type of gardening you plan to do, it is useful, not to say vital, to know what type of soil you have, as the soil make-up has an impact on how well different plants will grow. There are five main types of soil (shown here). However, it's possible to have a mixture of soils, say peaty loam or sandy clay, and different types within one garden.

① Sandy soil feels gritty, like seaside sand. A handful of it will pour out between your fingers because it's usually dry and loose-textured.

② Clay soil forms sticky, heavy lumps when it's wet and is hard and solid when it's dry.

③ Chalky soil is usually full of lumps of chalk, which crumble if you rub them together. It has a loose texture, making it easy to dig.

④ Loam is even-textured, feels soft and is a mid- to dark brown. It can be squeezed into a ball but is easily rubbed into crumbs again.

⑤ Peat is very dark and open-textured, almost like a sponge. It holds onto water well, but can be rather crumbly and difficult to re-wet when it does dry out.

# Preparing your plot

All plants grow better in well-prepared soil, and fruit trees and bushes are no exception. Although you can grow traditional-sized fruit trees and nut trees in grass, dwarfing varieties and those trained into fans, cordons and so on are much better without the competition. Soft fruits, fruit bushes and bedding fruits, such as rhubarb and strawberries, must have fertile, weed-free beds.

**Don't forget**

When clearing a lawn to create a new bed for fruit, stack removed turves upside down in a corner of your garden and over 18 months or so the grass will rot away and you can then recycle the soil back into your garden.

## Eradicating weeds

If you're creating a new bed or beds for your fruit plants, first remove the grass and any weeds. Skim the turf off with a spade in slices about 4cm (1¾in) thick so you get most of the roots too. With rough or overgrown ground, dig out perennial weeds and tree seedlings as well as any annual weeds that have set seed; dig smaller, non-seeding annual weeds back in.

Ideally, once it's dug over, you need to leave the ground alone for several months so that you can remove new weeds as they grow. Fork over the area occasionally to bring dormant weed seeds to the surface, where sunlight triggers them to germinate. Hoe these off or use a flame-gun on them before they have time to set seed or become established.

## Applying weedkiller

There's a lot to be said for using weedkiller to clear a very overgrown plot, but it takes time to do the job properly, and you must accept that this is not an organic solution.

Choose a total, non-residual weedkiller, such as glyphosate, and use it according to the manufacturer's instructions. Apply it on a still day (so you don't get uncontrolled drift) in late spring or early summer, when the weeds will be growing strongly.

Glyphosate is absorbed through the leaves and slowly kills the roots, so it'll be a week or two before the plants start dying off. When this happens you can clear the remains away. Wait four to six weeks and if regrowth occurs, repeat the

Use a rake to level the cultivated soil, once it has been broken down with a fork. Use firm, regular strokes to produce a level surface. Over-raking will cause the surface to form a crust, which may not drain well.

Clearing weeds and getting the ground ready for planting is a key starting point for a successful fruit garden. It is also very satisfying. Lighter soils can be dug with a spade, but a fork is easier to use on heavier or stony soils.

When you're preparing a bed for planting, add plenty of well-rotted compost. It's almost impossible to use too much organic matter: plants and soil organisms benefit from its nutrients, and it improves soil drainage and water-retaining ability.

treatment. Allow the weeds to grow a few centimetres high, so that there's enough foliage to absorb the product, but not so much that they regain their strength. Long-established colonies may need three or four treatments. Allow six to eight weeks after apparent death to be absolutely certain of eradication before cultivating the area.

## Soil improvement

Adding organic material, such as well-rotted manure or compost, to soil will improve its growing abilities, whether it's a heavy or a light soil. Dig in as much as possible. Your fruit is going to be growing in it for a long time, and you want it to have a really good start. If you've only just begun gardening and haven't got any of your own compost, phone around local stables or smallholders to see if they have any organic material to spare. Don't use spent mushroom compost, because it tends to be too alkaline for fruit.

If you have heavy, clay soil, consider adding plenty of sand or grit, as this will open up the soil structure, preventing it from baking too hard and improving aeration and drainage when it's wet.

## Making your own garden compost

It's really very easy to make your own compost. First, you'll need a compost bin – these are available in all shapes, sizes and materials; alternatively, you can make your own bin from wooden pallets and upright battens. The main rules when making compost are as follows:

■ Almost any kitchen or garden waste can be used, except cooked food and meat. Don't include cat or dog muck.

■ Use plenty of different materials, for example fine and coarse waste such as grass and potato peelings, and dry and wet waste such as unprinted paper and cardboard and annual weeds and plant trimmings.

■ Include worms and other organisms in the mixture to help the decaying process.

■ Woody material can take a long time to break down, so it's worth shredding stems and branches first (see page 23).

■ Mix the materials as you add them, to speed up the rotting process; alternatively, turn the heap once or twice before using the compost. If you've used woody material, you may have to do this more often.

■ Ideally, have three compost bins: one for material that is rotting down, one that you add to as you go along, and one that is ready for use.

Almost anything green can go into a compost bin, but avoid adding weed roots and seeds, as they will make new weeds. Annual weeds that haven't gone to seed are fine.

Once the bin is full, close the lid and leave the waste to rot down. In warm weather, the level inside the bin will go down considerably in just a few days.

# Choosing and planting fruit

It's usually recommended that trees and bushes are planted from autumn to spring, but not during very cold spells when the ground may be too hard to dig. However, with pot-grown specimens you can plant at any time, so long as you water well and regularly. Bare-rooted specimens are available only in the autumn, so that's when you need to plant them.

## Choosing and planting fruit trees and bushes

Fruit trees and bushes are usually sold in pots, although many nurseries will sell fruit trees bare-rooted, especially if you buy in bulk. When buying, choose with care. Although careful pruning will gradually improve appearance, the overall shape of a tree will remain much the same throughout its life, so don't pick something with a bent or damaged trunk, or with thick healthy branches on one side and spindly ones on the other. Bushes should be upright and evenly branched all around; their shape is more easily rectified by pruning, but why start off with second best?

Also check that the plant isn't pot bound. Do this by carefully easing off the container. Thin, fine roots

### Don't forget

Newly planted trees and shrubs need regular watering until they've put their roots down. If planting a fruit tree or bush during very dry weather it's worth filling the planting hole with a couple of buckets of water before planting and backfilling.

## HOW TO plant a fruit tree or bush

**1** Dig a hole about 1.2m (4ft) across in which to plant the tree or bush – it should be at least four times the diameter of the original pot, or its rootball if you bought a bare-rooted tree. Make the hole about one and a half times the depth of the pot. With a bare-rooted tree, there will be a mark where the soil level was before the tree was harvested. Make sure your hole is one and a half times that depth.

**2** Water the plant thoroughly about an hour before planting. Add garden compost or any other organic matter (such as a couple of bucketfuls of well-rotted manure) to the base of the hole and fork over the soil to mix it in. Also fork organic matter into the soil that you have removed from the hole. The idea is to have a good, moisture-retentive mix in which to plant your tree or bush, not simply garden soil.

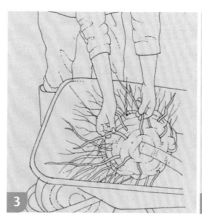

**3** If the tree's or shrub's roots have filled the pot, tease them out a bit all around to encourage them to break out from the pot shape and grow into the soil around them. Place the tree or shrub centrally in the hole, adding some of the compost–soil mixture if necessary to bring the top of the rootball just about level with the soil surface. Backfill around the rootball with the soil and compost mixture, then firm it in. Avoid firming on top of the rootball, as this can cause damage.

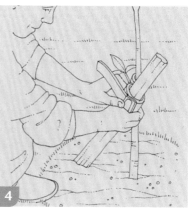

**4** Most trees need a stake for the first couple of years while they're rooting. Bush fruit are pruned after planting, so staking isn't necessary. Making sure you miss the rootball, hammer in a stake of about 1–1.2m (3–4ft) long. With pot-grown trees, angle it at 45 degrees to the ground with the top facing in the direction of the prevailing wind. Bare-root trees should be supported with a vertical stake. Make sure the stake is near enough to the tree to secure it with a proper tree tie.

should be just about filling the pot but there must still be compost visible all around; if there are thick, twisted roots around the edge of the rootball, choose another plant. Pot-bound plants are more difficult to establish as the roots tend to continue growing in on themselves, and they will have suffered from a lack of nutrients, so are likely to be less robust.

At least an hour before planting, give plants a very good soaking and immerse the roots of bare-rooted specimens in a bucket of water. Both bare-root and pot-grown trees can be planted in much the same way (*see* opposite).

## Planting against a wall or fence

The main thing to remember when planting any sort of plant near a wall or fence is that you're providing them with support and protection at the expense of water and, possibly, root space; and the very fact that they're protected by the wall or fence means they will be warmer and will need more water. You will have noticed that walls and fences tend to create a 'rainshadow', meaning that the area just beside them is very dry because it gets very little water.

For fruit trees and bushes, cane fruit and climbing fruit there are three key ways of improving the situation. First, you should plant them a little way out from the wall and train them back towards it (*see* above). Planting just a foot or so from the wall increases the plant's access to rainwater and prevents all your additional watering from going directly into the wall's foundations,

Plant climbers and trained trees and bushes about 25–30cm (10–12in) from the base of the wall or fence and guide the stems to the support. Passionfruit (*shown above*) have flexible stems, so attach them to a cane leaning towards the wall to prevent the plant from slumping.

which will eagerly suck it up. Secondly, before you plant you must add masses of organic matter to the soil all around the plant to increase its water-retaining potential. Finally, you must cover the soil with a thick mulch after planting (*see* page 40). Even if you do all these things, you'll still need to be assiduous in your watering.

The technique for planting is very similar to that for planting a freestanding tree, but to make life easier have all your supports in place before planting (*see* pages 30–1). With climbers and cane fruits, which have flexible stems, you can position

the rootball in the hole at a slight angle towards the wall or fence, so that the plant is already leaning in the right direction, but ensure that the soil level remains close to what it was in the pot. Once they're planted, secure the plants to their supports, water in well and mulch.

## Planting strawberries and rhubarb

Strawberries often come as bare-rooted plants, while rhubarb is readily available as roots; both are also sold in pots. Planting is similar for both bare-rooted and pot-grown plants, but with bare-rooted strawberries it is advisable to soak the roots for half an hour or so before planting. If you have a bundle, soak them before separating the plants out. Rhubarb is tougher, but even so, choose your roots with care; preferably pick one that has at least one obvious and plump bud. If very dry, they may not survive.

Prepare the planting area well, digging deeply all over, removing weeds and adding plenty of organic matter (*see* page 27), particularly for rhubarb. For strawberries, if you have heavy soil plant on top of ridges or mounds 8–10cm (3–4in) high, as this provides a little more drainage.

Dig a hole slightly larger than the pot, or the bundle of roots, and place the plant in it. It's important to keep the soil level the same as it was in the pot, especially with strawberries as they are prone to rotting if the crown (the bit where the shoots meet the roots) is planted too deeply. Replace the soil around the plants, press it down firmly and water in well.

Depending on how you grow them, fruit trees, climbers and canes need support for some or all of their lives. The better they're supported, the easier it is to care for them and therefore the more likely it is that you'll get a decent crop. For this reason, it's well worth spending a bit of time getting the right supports in place and making sure that they're adequate for the job.

## Stakes and posts

In their early years, freestanding trees need staking (*see* page 28). This prevents them from blowing about in the breeze, which would keep moving the roots around, breaking them and preventing establishment. Check stakes on a regular basis, loosening and adjusting the ties as necessary. Trunks can grow very quickly and it's terrible to find that a tie has garrotted your precious plant. After a couple of years, once the tree is growing strongly, the stake can be removed.

The posts of a pergola or an arch make the perfect support for vines, many cane fruit and other climbers, including kiwis and passionfruit; raspberries can also be grown around single posts. Make sure the structure is strong enough to support the weight of the plant as it grows, and drive individual posts at least 30cm (12in) into the ground. It's worth knocking in wire staples at regular intervals up and around posts to provide convenient anchors for the string or wire to which you'll tie your plants.

## Posts and wires

A system of horizontal wires is the traditional way to support raspberries (*see* opposite and pages 110–11), blackberries, grapes, kiwis and cordon, espalier and fan-trained fruit trees. The most sensible way to keep these in place is to have upright posts at regular intervals of about 3–4m (10–13ft),

depending on the space available. In the open, knock the posts well into the ground and attach strong wires between them. Once the fruit plants are trained on them, they will carry quite a lot of weight so the posts need to be sturdy. They're best set into concrete, or you could use post fixings, which are widely available.

If you're training fruit against a wall or fence, you can simply fix vine-eyes into the mortar between the bricks (*see* below) or into the upright fence posts, and secure wire between them. This will provide support for lighter plants, and may be suitable for trained trees and bushes too. However, if you're in doubt about the strength of your mortar, attach wooden posts to the wall and

Grapes are traditionally trained on a system of wooden posts and strong wires. There is a post for each plant and the first and last posts in each run are supported with angled props.

## HOW TO attach plants to walls using wires

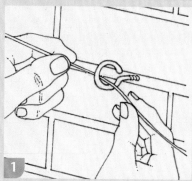

**1** Drill holes for the vine-eyes. Insert wall plugs into the holes and screw in vine-eyes at intervals along the wall. At one end, secure the wire around a vine-eye and then run it through the middle ones.

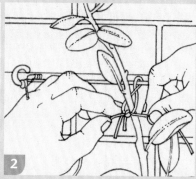

**2** At the other end, tension the wire around the final vine-eye, using pliers if needed. Tie in the fruit plant using soft twine or proprietary plant ties. Make the ties firm but not too tight around the stems.

screw the fixings into these. For most plants, space the wires about 30–45cm (12–18in) apart, starting 30cm (12in) above the ground. If you buy trees that are part-trained as espaliers or fans, fix wires at distances to coincide with the existing branches.

## Trellis

Trellis makes a very effective support for passionfruit and kiwis, as well as blackberries and other cane fruit. There is a wide range of designs, from the traditional wooden grid type to metal and wire sorts in many different shapes and sizes. Choose something that's big enough to support your plant when it's mature, and fix it to a wall or fence, or freestanding posts, using nails or screws. Bear in mind that the fully grown plant will be heavy, especially when wet or blown around by wind.

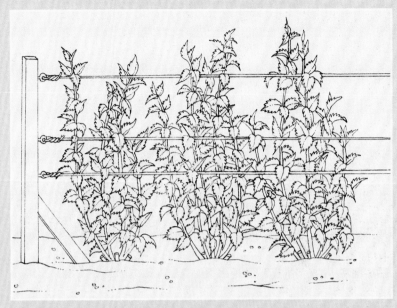

Raspberries and other cane fruit can be supported using posts set at intervals of about 4m (13ft). Screw vine-eyes into the posts and run wire through them. It's important that the wires are fixed firmly in place; if you like neatness, you can tension them as well. Tie in each cane, stem or branch using twine or thin wire.

Here, mature espalier apples are growing on posts and wires. Trained trees usually need permanent support, because their unnatural shapes make them vulnerable to damage by the wind or even a heavy crop.

# Growing fruit in containers

With the notable exception of raspberries, the majority of fruit can be grown in containers. Indeed, pot culture is so popular that tiny apples, plums, cherries and pears have been bred specifically for the purpose. Although such varieties will not produce the yields of those grown in the ground, they're a very good option for ambitious fruit growers with limited space or unsuitable soil.

Citrus fruit such as lemons look very handsome in large tubs or planters in the garden or a sunny courtyard. In fact, they must be grown in containers as they need to be moved indoors for the winter months. Their glossy leaves make them attractive to look at, even when not in flower or fruit.

The key to success with fruit in containers is to give them the best possible growing conditions. This means that you must select good-quality compost, use large pots, water and feed regularly and well, and repot (or root prune) as soon as it becomes necessary. Adequate support and careful pruning are also vital.

## Choosing compost

Most fruit trees and bushes should be grown in John Innes No. 3 potting compost with some grit and multipurpose compost added. The John Innes compost is loam-based; the loam retains nutrients for longer than normal potting compost and provides weight, which will prevent the pot being blown over during windy weather. The multipurpose compost is light and soft-textured, opening up the mixture and improving moisture retention, while the grit helps drainage and adds weight too. A good combination is equal parts John Innes and multipurpose compost with about one part grit; combinations of John Innes and multipurpose compost are now available at garden centres.

Blueberries and cranberries need acidic conditions, so replace the multipurpose compost with ericaceous compost for blueberries and use only ericaceous for cranberries, though still add the grit in both cases.

### Don't forget

When buying ericaceous compost for acid-loving plants, such as blueberries and cranberries, look for peat-free mixes, which are more environmentally friendly.

Put in a layer of crocks or stones. Make a 50:50 mix of John Innes No. 2 and multipurpose potting compost and fill the pot as far as the first planting hole.

Water the young plants thoroughly, then gently push the rootballs through the pot's planting holes. Lightly firm the compost around each rootball.

Plant the top of the pot and add more compost until it is about 5cm (2in) below the rim. Water well and place the pot in a sunny, sheltered site.

## Potting up

For trees, bushes and climbers, choose the largest pot you can cope with; it should be at least 38–45cm (15–18in) across at the top so you can repot easily. For strawberries, the pot can be as small as a hanging basket in which you could put three plants; but a larger container, say 25–30cm (10–12in), could take five plants while a large trough, say 60cm (2ft) long and about 25cm (10in) wide, would be fine for six or seven plants. Glazed pots retain moisture better than terracotta ones, so if you suspect watering might be a problem, select accordingly.

To ensure good drainage, put some pieces of broken terracotta pot in the bottom of the container or a layer of stones or gravel. Next, add some of your compost mixture to the pot so that when you insert your plant its rootball sits about 2.5–5cm (1–2in) below the pot rim. Measure your plant against the pot if necessary, or do it by trial and error. The main thing is to ensure you don't put in too much compost, because it's very difficult to water a pot if the compost is level with its rim.

Once the plant is in position, fill around the edges with your compost mixture, pushing it down the sides to get rid of air gaps and firming it in well as you go. Water the whole lot really well, to settle all the compost down around the roots. Finally, add a mulch of gravel or chippings. As well as looking decorative, these stop weeds from growing on the surface, prevent it from baking hard (which makes watering difficult) and reduce water evaporation.

## Watering and feeding

Water is very important to a growing plant; it is even more important to a plant in fruit. In summer you may need to water daily.

From April to mid-August, you also need to feed your plants once a week, as the nutrients provided in the original compost will soon be used up. Most fruit is fine with liquid tomato feed, diluted as recommended for tomatoes. Blueberries and cranberries are best fed with specialist feeds designed for lime-haters. Two or three times during this period, it's worth giving all pot-grown fruit an additional boost with seaweed extract. This provides trace elements and generally keeps them healthy. (For more information on watering and feeding, see pages 38–9).

### Don't forget

The difference between John Innes No. 2 and John Innes No. 3 is in the concentration of nutrients. John Innes No. 2 has slightly fewer nutrients and so is more suitable for smaller, less hungry plants such as strawberries. John Innes No. 3 is better for fruit trees and bushes.

## Other maintenance tasks

In winter, move fruit in pots to a sheltered spot out of the wind and away from the worst of the weather. Stand them on bricks or pot feet to prevent them from becoming waterlogged, but check them weekly to ensure they aren't totally dry either. If icy weather is forecast, wrap fleece, bubble wrap or hessian around the pots to stop them freezing. Grouping pots together helps insulation, or you could move them under cover – into a garage or shed perhaps – for a few days.

## Top-dressing and repotting

In spring, top-dress the plant. Carefully remove the chipping mulch, if you've used one, then scrape away the top 5cm (2in) of compost and replace it with new. You might have to cut through surface roots to do this, but don't worry, they'll soon be replaced. Fill up to the original level using the same mixture as before but with the addition of some slow-release fertilizer pellets this time as the volume of new stuff won't contain enough on its own to keep the plant healthy for long.

Every four or five years the plant will need repotting (*see* right). Either put it into a slightly larger pot, or prune off the outer 5cm (2in) or so of the rootball and put it back in the same pot.

**Don't forget**

With a chipping mulch on top of the compost, weeds should not be much of a problem, but if you spot any do remove them right away because they will compete with your fruit plant for nutrients and water.

## HOW TO repot a container-grown tree

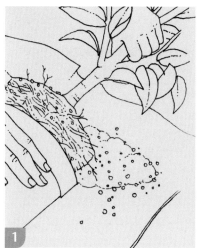
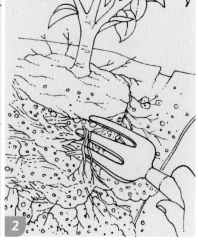

**1** Lay the plant on its side and gently remove the pot. If the plant is wedged firmly, loosen the rootball by tapping the container rim with a block of wood or slide a long knife between the pot and the compost.

**2** Using a hand fork, gently prise out any congested roots so that they can grow into the surrounding compost once replanted in the new container. Any thick roots that will make repotting difficult can be shortened.

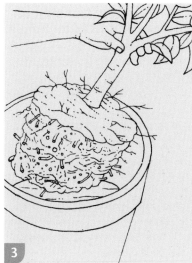

**3** Prepare the new, slightly larger pot for planting. Place a layer of mesh then crocks at the base of the pot, covering the drainage hole, then add a layer of compost to cover this. Place the plant in the centre of the pot, spreading out the roots if necessary.

**4** Fill the gap between the pot and the plant with more compost, easing it down the sides with your fingers and firming lightly. When potting is complete, the surface of the rootball should be approximately 2.5–5cm (1–2in) below the rim of the pot to allow for watering.

## Supporting plants

Provide climbers and fruiting canes with good, solid supports to clamber on (*see* pages 30–1). In most cases it's best to position the pots next to a wall or fence and attach trellis or wire supports to that, but you can grow a grapevine on a circular frame attached to a short stake (*see* below right) and keep the plant small through careful pruning of the rod-and-spur variety (*see* pages 71–2). A passionfruit can be trained on a large obelisk or wigwam, as long as you're prepared to keep hacking it back.

Bushes grown in pots usually don't require support. Trees may need a short stake initially if they have a very slender trunk (*see* below), but this isn't always needed since they won't grow as fast or as large as they would in the open ground, and their roots will quickly fill the pot so there isn't the same wind-rock problem. However, ballerina or pillarette/

minarette types (*see* pages 20–1) are comparatively tall and slender and need a permanent stout stake and two ties, one about halfway up and the other near the top. Place the stake in the pot at the same time as you plant the tree.

The main problem with larger plants in pots is top-heaviness. Get around this by selecting containers with a wide base and putting weighty crocks in the bottom before planting. If you still have trouble, wedge the pot between bricks or among other containers; alternatively, position the pot near a wall or fence to which you can attach a tie or two, or place it in or beside a flower bed, drive a stake into the soil and tie the tree to this.

These two pear trees, one a double cordon, are producing a healthy crop in patio pots that have been brightened with summer bedding.

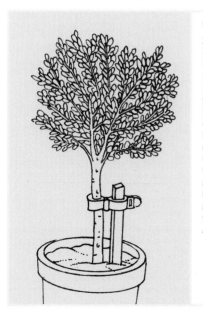

With slender or young pot-grown trees it is as well to provide a short, sturdy stake. This prevents the top-growth from blowing about and unbalancing the pot and stops a thin trunk from breaking. Attach the tree to the stake using a buckle-and-spacer tie. Taller trunks may need a second tie.

With careful training, a grape-vine can do well in a large pot and will produce four or five bunches of grapes. Grapes seem not to mind being restricted in this way. The main challenge is to get the watering right, otherwise the plants will get too dry and you tend to get powdery mildew.

# Growing fruit under cover

Many types of fruit can be grown in the shelter of a greenhouse, polytunnel, conservatory or even in a cold frame. In cold regions this may be the only way of ensuring you get any sort of crop, while in milder areas the extra warmth the cover provides will give a higher yield. Melons, citrus fruit, grapes, kiwis, passionfruit and figs are all obvious candidates, but you could also try peaches and nectarines as well as apricots if you experience late frosts.

**Don't forget**

If you want some early strawberries, pot up a few plants into a tub or container and bring them under cover at the end of summer. They will flower earlier the following year and the additional warmth brings earlier fruit, too.

## Planting under cover

Most plants under cover will be grown in pots (see pages 32–5). However, in polytunnels and greenhouses that have soil borders you'll make life easier for yourself if you plant directly into the soil. A traditional method of planting grapes was to have the roots outside in the garden and train the top of the plant into the conservatory or greenhouse. Few of us have the luxury of the space required for this, but the benefits are obvious: the plant roots can grow as much as they need to support the vigorous top-growth, they have access to nutrients in the soil and they get rainwater, so reducing the need for watering. Planting in a greenhouse or polytunnel border goes some way to meeting these requirements too, though you will have to water.

If you're planning to grow your plants in the soil, dig it over and add plenty of organic matter, just as you would in an outdoor planting site, and add a handful of slow-release fertilizer (see pages 38–9). Make sure your supports are in place where necessary (see pages 30–1) and before planting add a couple of buckets of water to the planting hole to ensure the soil is really damp. Now you can plant as you would normally (see pages 28–9), but bury an empty plastic soft-drinks bottle, spout end into the soil with the bottom cut off, next to the plant. When it comes to watering, gently pour the water into the improvised funnel; that way it goes directly to the roots, which are also encouraged to grow more deeply into the soil to find water.

## Watering

Water is the main thing that plants under cover cannot get naturally, so during the growing season (April to September) they'll need checking daily and in all probability will need watering almost daily. So much watering will flush nutrients out of the soil, particularly in pot-grown plants, so feed them at least fortnightly (see pages 38–9). Never

Peaches can do magnificently under cover, where conditions are more protected and considerably warmer than they are outdoors in the garden. This peach tree, which is the variety 'Peregrine', has produced so much fruit that it needs plenty of support with a network of wires.

Greenhouses can become very warm and dry during hot weather, which encourages pests and diseases. Damping down involves pouring water on the greenhouse floor to humidify the air and cool it too.

Too much sun shining through greenhouse glass can cause scorching on plant leaves. A shade paint applied to the outside of the glass reduces glare as well as the overall temperature inside the greenhouse.

## Pollination

Fruit grown under cover, especially types that flower very early in the year, such as peaches, apricots and nectarines, are at risk of not being pollinated either due to a lack of insects or those insects that are around not being able to get at the flowers. To ensure pollination you need to do it yourself. Use a small, soft paintbrush and gently brush it over the anthers of each flower, thus transferring the pollen from one flower to the next.

water mindlessly though, as it's quite easy to kill plants with too much water, particularly indoors where the roots can cook in a combination of water and heat. Pay attention to the needs of individual fruits – citrus require a good soaking about once a week and should be allowed to dry out almost entirely in between, while melons like plenty of water, although too much will cause the stems to rot at the bases (*see* under individual plants in the A–Z of fruit for more details, pages 74–115).

## Shade and ventilation

The extra heat is the main reason why we grow plants under cover, but during very hot spells it can cause the plants stress and encourage pests and diseases. Greenhouses can be shaded using a proprietary shade paint (*see* above centre), which reduces heat without blocking out too much light; it's easy to apply but a bore to remove at the end of the summer. Alternatively, you could use blinds. These reduce light and are easy to put up and remove, but are less efficient at reducing heat and are a little more costly than shade paint.

In addition, you'll need to open the doors and all the ventilators on hot days and damp down the floor by sprinkling it with water up to three times a day in the height of summer (*see* above left). Damping down also increases humidity, which keeps pests such as red spider mite at bay. It's usually more difficult to keep conservatories cool, especially if you're away during the day. Polytunnels do not need shading and tend to be quite humid, too, but damping down is still necessary.

## Winter care

Most fruits grown under cover are naturally deciduous and become dormant in winter. As the leaves begin to die in autumn, reduce watering, clear up fallen leaves and carry out normal pruning routines (*see* pages 54–73), then simply check the plants regularly to ensure they're not bone dry. Melons are annuals, so die off once they have finished fruiting. Citrus plants are evergreen and need some warmth in the winter – at least 10°C (50°F) – so are best in a heated greenhouse or conservatory; passionfruit are also evergreen but need no heat over winter. As fruit growth starts again in spring, increase watering, top-dress pot-grown plants (*see* page 34) and dig some slow-release fertilizer into the top few inches of the greenhouse border soil.

# Regular maintenance

Once your fruit is planted, all the necessary stakes, ties and supports are in place and everything is growing nicely, you can relax – but not for long. While you're still brimful of enthusiasm, it's a good idea to get into a routine that will ensure the garden stays in prime condition. Top of the list are watering and feeding, closely followed by regular weed control.

## Watering

All newly planted fruit needs frequent, thorough watering until it has become established. You can tell when this is the case as the plants will start to grow away more rapidly – it takes a couple of months for most types, depending on when they were planted. Autumn-planted fruit will be established by the spring and may need no special watering except in very dry periods; fruit that is planted in spring or later is much more vulnerable to drought and is best watered regularly for the whole of its first season. After this, you can prioritize watering fruit in the open garden, as follows:

**Strawberries** These small plants have shallow roots and are the first to suffer from dry spells, even very early in the growing season. Water two or three times weekly.

**Rhubarb, cane fruit, bush fruit and vines, trained and dwarf fruit trees** These need watering thoroughly once a week during prolonged dry weather. Pay particular attention to those that are growing against walls.

**Trees** Well-established trees can cope with drought; water only if they seem to be suffering. If this is a regular occurrence, look for a reason, such as a hedge competing for moisture or grass choking the trunk, and try to resolve it. Apply mulch in the spring to reduce water evaporation (*see* page 40).

## Feeding

Feeding is essential if you want a really good crop. Fruit plants work very hard through the spring and summer and appreciate the extra help – the reward will be better yields of more tasty fruit. It's also important to plant them into fertile, well-prepared soil in the first place (*see* pages 24–7).

### Slow foods

Fertilizers that are added to the soil before planting are in the form of pellets, powders or granules; these break down slowly in the soil so the growing plants can make use of them as needed.

### General-purpose fertilizers

These provide a range of nutrients, containing roughly equal quantities of NPK (*see* box, opposite). Rake them into the soil when you're preparing the site and fork them into the soil in and around each planting hole before planting. General-purpose fertilizers can also be used to provide your fruit with a

Water butts come in a variety of sizes and designs. Choose one to suit your garden and it will really look the part.

pick-me-up each spring. Follow the instructions on the packet, but as a rough guide use about a handful per square metre (10 square feet).

### Nitrogen-rich fertilizers

Chicken manure pellets, hoof and horn and seaweed meal are rich in nitrogen, which helps leafy growth. These are slow acting and should be applied as a general feed in early spring. Scatter them thinly around your plants and rake them in.

### Phosphate-rich fertilizers

Phosphate fertilizers encourage root growth. A blood, fish and bone feed is the best source of phosphate.

**Potash** Usually sold as sulphate of potash, this is given to encourage flowering and fruiting. The most commonly available types are not strictly organic, but specialist suppliers do sell organic potash.

## Fast foods

Along with the slow-release foods, most fruit plants benefit from some fast foods during the fruiting season. As they're applied with water, liquid or soluble feeds can be absorbed much more quickly, bringing almost instant results. There's a wide range available and it pays to spend a little time at the garden centre reading the labels to see what they all contain. Here are a few of the types of fertilizer available, both organic and inorganic:

**Seaweed extract** An organic and sustainable liquid feed, this is high in nitrogen (N) and trace elements (*see* box, below). It is used in a very diluted form and is a great tonic when sprayed onto plants as a foliar feed. However, it is quite pricey.

**Tomato feed** Although specifically formulated for tomatoes, this can be used on any fruiting plants. It's a good source of potash (K) and magnesium. Most makes are not organic, but organic versions are available from specialist suppliers.

Tomato fertilizer is a balanced feed that is ideal for the whole range of fruit-producing plants.

**General-purpose feed** Higher in nitrogen (N) than potash (K), this is intended for use on leafy crops and will not help fruit production. Use it sparingly, and only if your plants are in need of a tonic, otherwise you'll get leaf production at the expense of fruit. Really, it's better to apply slow-release fertilizers in spring (*see* opposite). Specialist suppliers will stock good organic alternatives.

**Fish emulsion** An organic product with an NPK of 5-2-2, plus trace elements, fish emulsion is used very diluted. It releases its nutrients quickly and is a great tonic early in the growing season.

### Understanding feed labels

The three most important plant nutrients are nitrogen (N), phosphate (P) and potash or potassium (K). There are also plenty of other trace elements that a plant finds useful.

The container in which you purchase any fertilizer will show the proportions of NPK it contains, as well as any trace elements (or micronutrients), such as boron (B), copper (Cu), iron (Fe), manganese (Mn), chlorine (Cl) and zinc (Zn). Don't worry about all this – all you really need to know is the proportions of NPK in a fertilizer and what these do for your plants.

## Weeding

Because fruit plants mostly look big and tough compared to, say, vegetables, it's easy to think that a few weeds around them won't be a problem. However, do not be fooled – weeds are thieves of food, water, light and space and harbourers of pests and diseases, so they will always be a disadvantage to any cropping plants.

### Taking care of weeds

The first thing to do is to prepare your fruit garden well before planting (*see* pages 26–7) – this way, weeds will be less of a problem. Next, remove weeds sooner rather than later, and the job will take no time at all. Annual weeds and small perennial weeds can be dealt with by hoeing, larger perennial weeds may take more effort.

While the weed seedlings are tiny, hoe every week or two. For best results, hoe on a dry, sunny day, and leave the weed seedlings to shrivel up in the sun. You need to be careful when hoeing around strawberries, as they're shallow-rooted; if you aren't adept with a hoe, use your fingers and a hand fork instead.

The best way to remove larger or established perennial weeds – which include bindweed, ground elder, dandelions, docks and stinging nettles – is to dig them up, roots and all. However, this is almost impossible to do. Most root very deeply and have brittle roots that annoyingly snap just below your trowel. Leaving just the bare minimum behind will enable them to regrow. Ideally, revisit each weed on a regular basis (weekly), removing all top-growth. This will weaken and eventually kill it. Otherwise, consider using a spot weedkiller. Based on glyphosate, this is painted or sprayed on the offending plant and nothing else. Be aware that glyphosate is capable of killing all plants, including those you want to keep, and it's not for organic gardeners.

## Using mulches

If you hate weeding, mulches are the answer, since they keep weeds down as well as creating much better growing conditions for your plants. Weeds will grow in the mulches, but they don't tend to root as deeply so are much easier to remove.

The soil needs to be moist when you spread the mulch, because besides inhibiting weeds, one of the main reasons for mulching is that it helps to keep the soil moist in summer by minimizing evaporation.

Each spring, remove any weeds from around the plants, water well if the weather has been dry (or wait until a wet spell and mulch afterwards) and then spread about 5cm (2in) or more of mulching material over all the exposed soil. Well-rotted manure or garden compost are the best mulches, but bark chippings (which last longer) are acceptable too. All these will rot down slowly, giving your plants some additional nutrition as well.

If you like to get ahead, you could spread your mulch any time from February onwards, but do get it done before mid-March, when fruit trees and bushes start coming into leaf or bloom, so there's less risk of damaging new growth as you work.

Among fruit, strawberries are most likely to suffer from competition from weeds. This is because they're low-growing and shallow-rooted. Hoe or hand-weed rows regularly, taking care around the roots. If your aim is not very good, use a hand fork or trowel and get down on your knees!

## Mulching strawberries

Strawberries should not be deeply mulched, since this will encourage moulds and rots, as well as harbouring slugs. There are several ways to keep weeds and pests at bay and prevent damp from rotting the fruit.

① Synthetic strawberry mulch mats protect plants from soil and rain splashes, retain moisture and warmth in the soil, and deter slugs.

② Straw is a natural alternative mulch for strawberries – place it under and around the plants as soon as the flowers are over.

# Propagation

Most fruit plants are quite straightforward to propagate. The exceptions are trees – some of these need to be grafted onto rootstocks while others would take years to reach fruiting age and so are not worth trying except for a bit of fun. Young strawberries and rhubarb, as well as cane fruit, will usually crop in the summer or autumn after they've been propagated, but with most other fruit it will be several years before you see the results of your work.

## Hormone rooting preparations

These are specially formulated to encourage cuttings to produce roots. They undoubtedly increase your chances of success with many plants, but some, particularly blackberries and related cane fruit, will root easily enough without help. Organic versions are available.

There are a number of ways and techniques used to propagate fruit, including layering, taking cuttings, sowing seed and division. (For information on how to propagate a particular type of fruit, *see* the chart on page 45.)

## Layering

Cane fruit, such as blackberries, will produce roots wherever their stems touch the ground; this is how brambles spread so effectively over large patches of ground. Layering is simply deliberately touching stems to the ground to get new plants on demand. To propagate by layering (*see* right), bend a stem to the ground and bury a short portion near its end under the soil. Ensure it doesn't spring back up when you let go by anchoring it (a loop of wire weighted down with a stone or brick does the job). Water during dry spells, otherwise leave the layer until you see new growth appearing. In the autumn or following spring, sever the new plant from its parent stem and pot it up.

For most plants, it's recommended that you make a small cut in the bark where the stem will come into contact with the soil, as this stimulates the roots to grow from this point.

## HOW TO propagate by layering

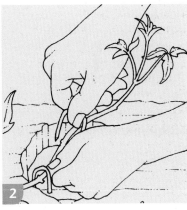

**1** Select a strong, healthy shoot from the plant you want to propagate, and strip off some of the leaves approximately 20cm (8in) behind the growing-tip.

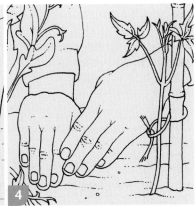

**2** Pull the shoot down to ground level and dig a small hole where the stem touches the soil. Make a small cut in the bark before burying it, to stimulate growth.

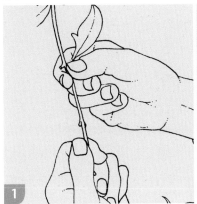

**3** To secure the stem, peg it down into the hole using a looped piece of wire. If necessary, tie the shoot-tip to a bamboo cane to keep it upright.

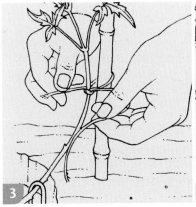

**4** Refill the hole with soil and firm it back down before watering thoroughly. After the plant has rooted, cut the new plant from its parent and pot it up.

## Taking cuttings

Taking cuttings can be an unpredictable business, but it is the best way to propagate a wide range of fruit plants, and is easy and fun to do. If you have a healthy plant, you can try taking a few cuttings at a time over several weeks, to ensure success. With semi-ripe and softwood cuttings, a heated propagator can increase your chances too. The rules to follow are simple:

■ Always use a sharp knife or secateurs to take cuttings. This avoids damaging the tissues that you want to produce roots.
■ The length of a cutting depends partly on the distance between leaf nodes. You need at least two nodes per cutting, one at the top to produce the leaves of the new plant, and one at the bottom to produce the roots.
■ Use cutting compost mixed with sharp sand or grit; for fruit that likes acid conditions, such as blueberries and cranberries, use ericaceous potting compost.
■ Make sure the compost is damp before inserting the cuttings and then don't water until you're sure they've produced roots. Water only if the compost has dried out.
■ Place cuttings in a sheltered, bright but not too sunny spot. Avoid placing them in direct sunlight.
■ Don't keep pulling on the cuttings to see whether they've rooted. They will take their time and this won't hurry them.

## Hardwood cuttings

Take hardwood cuttings in autumn (*see* right), using stems that are the current year's growth. Several cuttings can be made from one stem, so long as there is an embryo bud at the top and one at the bottom. Hardwood cuttings take several months to root. Do not disturb them until new growth appears and is well underway.

## Semi-ripe cuttings

Semi-ripe cuttings are made from stems that have grown this year and are just beginning to mature and harden. They're quicker to root than hardwood cuttings and less likely to wilt than softwood cuttings. Look

## HOW TO take hardwood cuttings

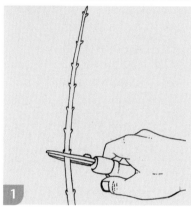

1 Remove a length of healthy stem from the current year's growth using secateurs. Make a straight cut just below a leaf bud. Remove any sideshoots.

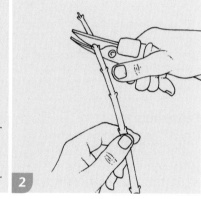

2 Trim the top of the cutting just above a leaf bud, so you have a length of stem 20–30cm (8–12in) or so long. Make a sloping cut.

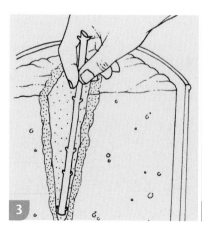

3 Insert the cutting, base first, to two thirds its depth in a trench outdoors in the vegetable patch, or else in a frost-resistant container filled with free-draining, moist cutting compost.

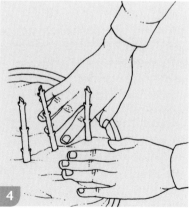

4 Continue inserting the cuttings, placing them in a row along the trench, firming the soil in around them as you go. Water well. Stand pots in a well-lit, frost-free, sheltered spot outside over winter.

for a length of stem that has begun to firm up at the base. If you find a suitable sideshoot, pull it gently away and downwards from the main shoot. This should peel a small amount of bark and tissue from the main shoot with it (a heel). Otherwise, take a length of shoot without a heel, called a stem-tip cutting. To take these, use a sharp knife to cut a shoot that is about 10cm (4in) long, with about 2.5cm (1in) of firm wood at the base.

With both types of semi-ripe cutting, remove the leaves from the lower end of the stem, leaving them on the top 2.5cm (1in). Fill a pot with damp cutting compost. Making holes with a pencil or piece of stick, put cuttings in around the rim of the pot. Cover the pot with a clear plastic bag, as with softwood cuttings (*see* right), and stand it in a light spot, out of direct sunlight.

Semi-ripe cuttings take about three or four months to root and can then be potted on separately.

## Softwood cuttings

Softwood cuttings (*see* right) are taken from the soft, new growth that appears at the beginning of a growing season. They should produce roots and grow away more quickly than semi-ripe and hardwood cuttings. However, because they're soft and sappy, they're also more vulnerable to damage and wilting.

### Don't forget

Dirty secateurs or knives can spread viruses from plant to plant. Always use clean tools and disinfect them if you've been removing diseased growth.

## Sowing seed

Most fruit produce seed, but because of all the breeding that has gone into our fruit, the plants that result from these seeds are unlikely to be anything like their parents, particularly in the fruit they produce.

However, alpine strawberries, melons and passionfruit can be raised from seed (indeed the first two must be raised from seed) with very good results. Some citrus can be raised from seed, with variable results, and nuts can also be raised

## HOW TO take softwood cuttings

**1** Cut several healthy shoots from the plant you wish to propagate (here, a blueberry plant). Each cutting should be about 8–10cm (3–4in) long.

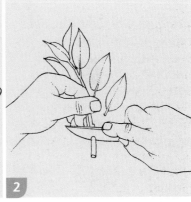

**2** Using a sharp knife, neaten the lower end of the stem, cutting just below a leaf joint. Leave two or three leaves at the top of the cutting, but remove the rest.

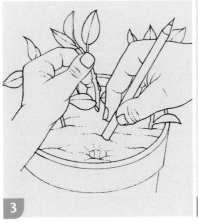

**3** Fill a pot with damp cutting compost. Making holes with a pencil or thin stick, insert the cuttings around the rim of the container. Don't push them in too far.

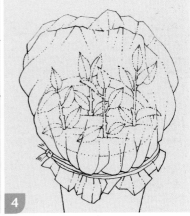

**4** Cover the pot with a clear plastic bag and hold it in place with string or an elastic band; the bag provides humidity. Stand the pot in a light spot, out of direct sun.

from seed. However, seed-raised trees take many years to fruit. (For How to sow seeds, *see* below.)

## Propagating by suckers, runners and division

These methods are easy and almost instant with a high success rate.

Plants such as raspberries and cobnuts naturally produce suckers, which are really only stems that grow out of the ground in the wrong place. Dig around these to expose the point where they're joined to the parent plant. Slice cleanly through this junction and then ease the sucker up, including as many roots as you can. Pot up or replant suckers straight away.

Strawberries produce runners as part of their growing cycle. These are long stems with one or, usually,

more little plantlets growing on them. Under the plantlet are some short, stubby, dry, root-like growths. These are waiting to root, so all you need to do is either pin the plantlet into place in the ground around the plant, or pin it into a small pot filled with potting compost and grit. (For How to propagate using runners, *see* page 115.)

Rhubarb is the only commonly grown fruit that is propagated by division. Dig up the rootball once the leaves have died back in late autumn and slice vertically through it using a sharp spade (*see* right). You can cut it into several pieces, depending on its size, making sure that each piece has a selection of healthy roots and at least one dormant bud. Replant or pot up all the pieces.

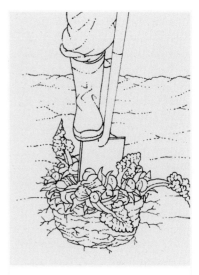

Rhubarb forms a dense, chunky rootball that can be sliced through to create new plants. As long as each piece has a leaf bud and some healthy roots it should quickly grow into a new plant.

## HOW TO sow seeds

**1** Fill a pot with seed compost and firm it down gently. Scatter small seeds (passionfruit and strawberry) onto the surface of the compost, ensuring thin, even distribution; push larger seeds (melon and citrus) into the compost.

**2** Sprinkle a thin layer of sieved compost over the seeds so that you cover them completely. Water well by standing the pot in a shallow tray of tepid water until the moisture has been absorbed and appears on the compost surface.

**3** Cover the pot with a clear plastic bag or put it in a heated propagator. Place it in a bright spot but not direct sunlight. If the compost is dry, water as previously. Once the seedlings appear, remove the plastic bag or remove from the propagator.

# How and when to propagate fruit

Many fruit can be propagated by straightforward means, usually by sowing seed or by taking cuttings. However, most fruit trees are grafted or budded onto special rootstocks (*see* page 15), methods that are generally beyond the scope of amateur gardeners.

| FRUIT | METHOD | SEASON | LENGTH OF CUTTING | NOTES |
|---|---|---|---|---|
| **Blackberries and their hybrids** | Layering | Late spring or early summer | Not applicable | The whole stem-tip can be covered and reappear above ground as the roots grow. |
| **Blackcurrants** | Hardwood cuttings | Autumn | 20–25cm (8–10in) | Insert cuttings in soil outdoors. |
| **Blueberries** | Softwood or semi-ripe cuttings | Late spring to midsummer | 8–10cm (3–4in) | Use ericaceous potting compost and a heated propagator. |
| **Citrus fruit** | Seed | Spring or summer | Not applicable | Citrus grown from seed will not always resemble the parent plant. |
| **Cranberries** | Semi-ripe cuttings | Late summer | 10–12cm (4–5in) | Use ericaceous potting compost and a heated propagator. |
| | Layering | Late spring or early summer | Not applicable | |
| **Figs** | Layering | Late spring or early summer | Not applicable | Fig cuttings can be slow to take. Be patient. |
| | Hardwood cuttings | Autumn | 30cm (12in) | |
| **Gooseberries** | Hardwood cuttings | Early autumn | 30–38cm (12–15in) | Remove any low sideshoots when the cuttings have rooted. |
| **Grapes** | Hardwood cuttings | Late autumn or winter | 20cm (8in) | Raise cuttings of indoor grapes in pots and outdoor grapes in the soil outdoors. |
| **Kiwi fruit** | Softwood cuttings | Spring | 10–15cm (4–6in) | Although you can grow kiwi plants from the tiny seeds, the resulting plant may not be a fruit producer (female) itself. |
| | Hardwood cuttings | Late summer | 20–30cm (8–12in) | |
| | Layering | Late spring or early summer | Not applicable | |
| **Melons** | Seed | Early spring | Not applicable | Use a heated propagator. |
| **Mulberries** | Hardwood cuttings | Autumn or early winter | 18cm (7in) | Mulberry roots are brittle, so take great care when potting up successful cuttings. |
| | Layering | Late spring or early summer | Not applicable | |
| **Nuts** (cobnuts and hazels) | Suckers | Winter | Not applicable | Suckers are the quicker option as you get a reasonable-sized plant instantly. |
| | Layering | Autumn | Not applicable | |
| **Passionfruit** | Seed | Spring | Not applicable | Use a heated propagator. |
| | Softwood or semi-ripe cuttings | Late spring to midsummer | 15–20cm (6–8in) | |
| **Quinces** | Softwood, semi-ripe or hardwood cuttings | Early summer, late summer or autumn | 20–23cm (8–9in) | Cuttings take several years to be mature enough to flower and fruit. Suckers are a quicker method. |
| | Suckers | Late autumn or early winter | Not applicable | |
| **Raspberries** | Suckers | Late autumn | Not applicable | Dig up a sucker and replant it. |
| **Redcurrants and whitecurrants** | Hardwood cuttings | Early autumn | 30–38cm (12–15in) | Remove lowest buds so the resulting plant has a short, branchless trunk or 'leg'. |
| **Rhubarb** | Division | Spring | Not applicable | Divisions propagate quickly. |
| **Strawberries** | Runners (most) | Autumn | Not applicable | Alpine varieties can only be propagated by seed; others only by runners. |
| | Seed (Alpine varieties) | Early spring | Not applicable | |

If you want to have fruit to eat, high on your list of considerations should be protecting your crop. Just as we find it difficult to resist tasting a strawberry, raspberry, apple or plum that is ripe and ready to eat, so do birds, slugs and a variety of insects. However, these are not the only enemy; early in the year, poor weather can cause problems. A serious fruit gardener needs to be prepared for every eventuality. (*See also* Pests and diseases, pages 50–3.)

### Don't forget

Horticultural fleece will provide protection against frost and also against damage caused by driving rain or strong winds, so it's useful for covering young crops any time these are forecast. Never wrap plants in plastic, because condensation builds up and might cause plants to rot; by contrast, fleece 'breathes'.

## Frost and cold weather

The plants that are particularly vulnerable to frost are those that are borderline hardy or those that flower early in the year. The early flowers may be killed by the frost, or damaged to the extent that pollinating insects are no longer interested in visiting them. A late frost can damage emerging leaves too, and while this is unlikely to be fatal, except in the very youngest of plants, it can set your plants back and reduce crops. On smaller trees and bushes, frost protection is very easy to provide. As frosts usually occur overnight, simply cover them with a piece of horticultural fleece any time frost is forecast (*see* below). The fleece can be removed during the day if it's warm enough, to allow insects to pollinate. Fleece is sold in garden centres and is inexpensive; in an emergency a net curtain, light tablecloth or old sheet will do, but be sure not to leave these on too long as they will tend to become wet and heavy from the frost, which fleece does not.

## Birds and other animals

Birds can be a bit of a nuisance to the fruit gardener, stripping overwintering buds off fruit trees and sampling your produce through the summer and into autumn. In many cases, netting is the best solution (*see* opposite). However, it may not be enough just to drape this over your plants, as the birds can reach through the netting and peck at the fruit. They can also get tangled up in loose netting, although this is less likely if you go for a heavy-duty option – don't buy the very light stuff, as it gets

During cold weather, it's easy to rig up a basic frame against a fence or wall and drape horticultural fleece over it. This simple shelter could mean the difference between a good crop and no crop.

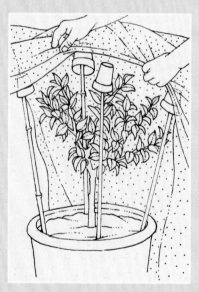

If cold weather is forecast, cover early-flowering, pot-grown fruit with fleece. Canes with small pots on the top will hold the fleece off the blossom, which might otherwise be damaged by damp.

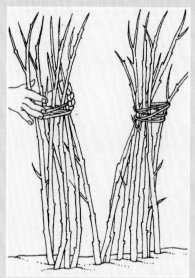

Cane fruit and currants are generally fairly robust, but even they will benefit from being tied up in a bundle to prevent damage from cold during particularly inclement weather.

There are various ways to protect fruit plants from birds.

① Chicken wire over strawberries is adequate defence against birds.

② Protect gooseberries using heavy-duty netting and tying it around the 'leg'.

## Fruit cages

Fruit cages are the very best option for protecting smaller fruit plants from predators and they will reduce wind and weather damage, too. However, they can be pricey and sometimes unattractive. They're available flatpacked from garden centres and mail-order suppliers and vary from around 1m (3ft) high, which is suitable for rows of strawberries, to 2m (6ft), which will accommodate most of your fruit, apart from larger trees. Alternatively, you could make your own fruit cage, using pressure-treated timber and heavy-duty netting.

When choosing a fruit cage, bear in mind the following:

■ It must be strong enough to withstand wind and weather.

■ It should be provided with suitable anchors to prevent it from blowing away.

■ If it's a walk-in type, the door needs to be a good size and easy to operate.

■ The netting gauge must be large enough to allow pollinating insects to enter and sufficiently heavy not to ensnare birds.

itself into a tangle whatever you do. Instead of draping, it's best to construct a framework of canes around the plants and hang the net over this, weighting down the bottom so birds can't get in that way either. Alternatively, tie or staple galvanized chicken wire onto the frame (see above).

If you have a problem with rabbits, deer or voles nibbling at the bark of your fruit trees, tree guards will deter them, but remember to check these regularly to ensure they're not restricting your tree's growth or causing damage through rubbing. They should also be removed occasionally. This is partly to discourage the populations of woodlice that tend to build up in them and also do some nibbling. In addition, it allows air to the trunk, which may otherwise become vulnerable to fungal diseases.

## Wind

Wind is a real enemy in the fruit garden, mainly because it discourages pollinating insects from going about their business, which means you'll get less fruit. On a cold day, wind can scorch the flowers, which makes them much less interesting to insects, and damage emerging leaves, so weakening the plant's growth. Wind continues to be a nuisance once fruit is set, as it can knock the fruit about, bruising it or making it fall before you're ready to pick it.

If your fruit garden is in a windy site, it's well worth considering putting in a windbreak on the most exposed side. A fence or a hedge will do the job very well. It's best to have a fence that is open in design, as this will slow the wind's progress, whereas a fully boarded fence will actually cause more turbulence on the leeward side.

Covering strawberries with a cloche – whether it's an old-fashioned barn cloche or a modern plastic type – will be rewarded by a delicious crop of early fruit.

# Harvesting and storage

Harvest is the time when all your dreams come to fruition and you can finally enjoy your hard-earned crops. Most fruit are best when eaten fresh, ideally within hours of picking – that is one of the reasons you grow them after all. If you must store fruit, there are ways and means, and even less-than-perfect produce can be used in cooking and for making jams.

Fruit gluts are a boon to a keen cook. Most fruit is delicious made into jams and several types can be combined for different flavours. Jam is very easy to make and home-made is much better than even the best shop-bought ones.

## Picking fruit

Believe it or not, there is a secret to picking – not in the technique exactly, but in the way the fruit looks, smells and comes off the plant, which will tell you whether it's ripe or not. Only with later-ripening apples and pears do you need to pick fruit before it's ripe and store it until it is ready to eat. The A–Z of fruit (see pages 74–115) gives more details about harvesting fruit, but here is a general guide.

## Colour and texture

The colour of most fruit changes to a warmer, richer shade as it ripens. With some soft fruit, such as raspberries and the currants, it's best to wait a day or two after they appear to have turned ripe so that the flavour can be allowed to develop completely.

Ripe fruit is softer than unripe fruit. In some cases, such as apples, the difference is hardly noticeable, but in others, for example plums, apricots, peaches and nectarines, there is a definite 'give' in the skin. It takes practice to get to know how this feels, but be gentle and don't go around squeezing all your fruit, as this will only cause bruising. There are exceptions – pears (see pages 105–6) and medlars (see page 109) are picked hard and kept until soft.

## Smell and pickability

If a fruit doesn't smell ripe, it isn't ripe. Leave it for another day.

Fruit that is ready for picking is pickable. It comes off the bush, tree or cane without a complaint – it wants to be eaten. Raspberries and

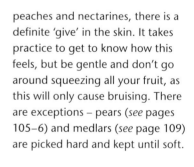

A ripe apple will come off the tree with the gentlest of twists. To avoid bruising, have a basket or box ready and treat each apple as if it were your only one.

blackberries, for example, simply slide off their inner core with the softest beckoning. If you need to pull, they aren't ripe. Again, there are exceptions, such as melons (*see* pages 97–8) and passionfruit (*see* page 102), which must be snipped off with a short stem to avoid damaging the rest of the plant.

## Storing fruit

Unless you have acres of land with large polytunnels full of soft fruit, it's unlikely that you'll have very much produce to store. And the general rule for most of us would be: don't do it. But, nevertheless, there are some types of fruit that lend themselves to storage, and while frozen raspberries, blackberries or gooseberries are not an exciting prospect in summer, when there are fresh ones around, they can be a real tonic in a crumble or fool in the dead of winter.

### Freezing

Choose the firmest, soundest fruit for freezing, and if you must wash it make sure it is thoroughly dry before you put it in the freezer. Spread out the fruit in a single layer on a clean tray and put it in the quick-freeze part of your freezer. As soon as it's frozen, put it in bags or plastic boxes.

Blackberries and their hybrids, blueberries, cranberries, currants, gooseberries, mulberries, raspberries and strawberries can be frozen as they are. Strawberries are the least successful, as freezing completely changes their character, causing them to become rather soggy.

Apricots, cherries, plums, peaches and nectarines can be frozen after

Pears and late-maturing apples must be picked before they're ripe, and then ripened under cover. These simple but effective storage racks are just what's needed and wouldn't be hard to construct if you're handy with a saw and hammer. The plastic bags prevent the skins from drying out and becoming wrinkled.

### Don't forget

Even if you choose perfect fruit, there's always the chance they will start to rot in the store. Check them over regularly and remove any that are starting to go soft before they affect the others around them.

the stones have been removed, which means they need stewing first. Blanch rhubarb before freezing.

Apples and pears are often frozen as part of a pre-cooked dessert, such as a pie or crumble, but they can also be frozen as purées.

### Making jams

The great thing about jam is that all the damaged and small fruit can go in and no one is the wiser. When properly made, jam is very tasty and has all the flavour of the original fruit, as well as being far superior to shop-bought stuff. Yes, it has sugar in it, but you don't have to eat it in great quantities.

Almost all fruit can be used to make jam, although apples and

pears are best combined with other fruit (otherwise all you get is a thick purée), or used in chutneys. The key to jam-making is pectin, which is the ingredient that makes jams set. Some types of fruit contain plenty of pectin and set easily, others need additional pectin. If you're new to jam-making, try the easy ones first; these include blackcurrants, redcurrants and gooseberries. Strawberries and blackberries are low in pectin.

### Apricot preserves

If you regularly produce huge crops of apricots that you can't use fresh, rather than freezing them take whole or halved fruits and preserve them in jars of sweetened brandy to eat at Christmas.

# Pests and diseases

Well-tended fruit trees, bushes, vines and other plants will be healthy and strong and so able to resist most pests and diseases. However, there are problems that seem to appear from nowhere and nearly always cause some consternation. In most cases a few simple changes to your cultivation techniques are all that's needed, but some pests and diseases are more threatening than others, and you may need to act promptly to save your crop or even your plants.

## Avoiding problems

Fortunately, there are plenty of ways to limit problems and reduce their impact. First and foremost is to keep your plants healthy by providing them with plenty of water and regular feeding and keeping weeds down. Healthy plants can cope with a few greenfly and will tend to shrug off fungal diseases before they take hold. It's also important to follow a sensible pruning regime, as this will remove dead and damaged branches that could allow diseases into your plants. If the pests can't get in, they can't hurt – this mostly applies to birds, which can cause havoc among your soft fruit in particular (*see* pages 46–7).

## Companion plants

Companion plants are a popular feature of vegetable gardens, where they're grown with the idea that they distract pests from the veg. There are various theories about how they work. One theory is that the pests find the companion plant more attractive than the veg; another is that they disguise the smell of some vegetables, effectively putting the pests off course. Among the key companion plants are herbs such as chervil, dill, hyssop, lavender and thyme – these produce a distracting scent and attract pollinators. Although less commonly practised in the fruit garden, the principles of companion planting are the same. Nasturtiums are thought to attract aphids away from strawberries and fruit trees. Strong-smelling herbs, such as chives, may deter wasps from eating plums.

### Biological controls

It's a rule of nature that most creatures have at least one predator. Scientists have developed ways of bringing the two together for the benefit of the gardener. The results are called biological controls and you can buy them from specialist suppliers. They work best in the greenhouse. Of those listed below, only the codling moth and slug nematodes are suitable for outdoor use.

| PEST | BIOLOGICAL CONTROL |
| --- | --- |
| Aphid | *Aphidius* species (parasitic wasp larva) |
| Codling moth caterpillar | *Steinernema carpocapsae* (nematode) |
| Red spider mite | *Phytosieulus persimilis* (predatory mite) |
| Slug | *Phasmarhabditis hermaphrodita* (nematode) |
| Vine weevil larva | *Steinernema kraussei* (nematode) |

A group of standard gooseberries is surrounded by a carpet of nasturtiums, which make a beautiful, weed-suppressing display. In addition, nasturtiums are believed to attract pests, such as aphids, away from crops.

# Know the enemy

There are a few pests and diseases that very commonly affect fruit. These are usually easily recognized, and if you act quickly can be simple to combat. Remember, though, that pests and diseases are a fact of life and do not always have to spell disaster. Some problems are more prevalent in particular areas or soils, or during some types of weather conditions. Most often, the damage they do is limited and you could simply resign yourself to sharing a proportion of your crops with them.

## Slugs and snails

These are a ubiquitous garden problem, but in the fruit garden they are only really annoying on strawberries, which they can eat completely overnight. Use a selection of the remedies below in and around your rows of strawberries, beginning a few weeks before the fruit ripens, to reduce numbers overall.

**Prevention and control**  Picking off by hand is effective, particularly with snails, but they must be destroyed; they will return if you simply throw them next door. Natural predators include thrushes, hedgehogs, newts, frogs, toads and ground beetles. Copper tape fixed to raised beds and containers will deliver a slight electric shock. Absorbent granules dehydrate slugs and snails so they can't glide along. Yucca extract or garlic-based deterrents taste bitter. Sharp grit and prickly leaves, such as holly, have a limited effect. Beer traps made from yoghurt pots or jam jars sunk into the ground are partially effective.

## Aphids

Greenfly and blackfly are mainly a spring problem. They're mostly found near the tips of soft young shoots and on the undersides of young leaves. A small infestation won't do much harm, but a larger one can weaken plants; they may also spread viral diseases. Particularly susceptible are pears, plums, peaches, nectarines, cherries (cherry blackfly), strawberries and all currants.

**Prevention and control**  Hand squash the aphids or blast them off with a hosepipe. Natural predators include blue tits and other birds, hoverflies, ladybirds, lacewings, spiders and several species of parasitic wasp, so encourage these into your garden. Spray with an insecticide if needed. Check to make sure it's suitable for edible plants.

## Caterpillars

Caterpillars are voracious feeders, and winter moth caterpillars are notorious for damaging the young leaves, flowers and buds of pears, plums and cherries, as well as the young, developing fruit.

**Prevention and control**  Check susceptible plants regularly and remove caterpillars or suspect clusters of eggs on the undersides of leaves by hand. Natural predators such as blackbirds and robins will take small caterpillars, and even wasps will do so early in the season. Trees can be protected by preventing the female from laying her eggs on them. This involves encircling the trunks with a sticky layer between late summer and early spring. Garden centres sell grease or sticky strips specially for this purpose. Insecticides may also be used at the first signs of attack.

## Red spider mite

Signs of red spider mite infestation include yellowing leaves, dusty webbing on the underside of leaves (this protects the breeding colonies) and stunted growth. Red spider mites are virtually invisible; don't mistake them for the larger red spiders, which are harmless. Red spider mite is an indication of low humidity levels and usually occurs under cover in greenhouses, polytunnels or conservatories; it can also affect fruit that is growing beside fences or walls, where conditions can be dry.

**Prevention and control** Increase humidity by spraying leaves and watering more frequently. Under cover you can use a biological control (*see* page 50). For heavy infestations, insecticide is an option.

## Wasps

Wasps bore into ripe fruit, particularly apples, pears, peaches, plums, figs and grapes, and can ruin a crop.

**Prevention and control** Pick ripe fruit daily and don't leave damaged, fallen or overripe fruit lying around. Hang up old-fashioned wasp traps. To make one, dissolve a teaspoonful of jam in a cup of warm water and pour the mixture into a jam jar. Put a circle of paper over the top of each jar, secured with an elastic band, and make a hole in the middle, only just big enough for a wasp to get in. Empty every few days when the fluid is full of wasps and start again.

## Bacterial canker

Bacterial canker can be very serious in cherries in particular, and can kill young trees. It also affects apples (which can also suffer from the somewhat similar Nectria canker, *see* page 76), plums, peaches, nectarines and apricots. The first symptoms are small, round, brown spots, then holes, in leaves. The following spring, buds fail to develop or stunted leaves appear and turn yellow and wither. Branches die back and oozing cankers form on the bark.

**Prevention and control** Remove dead and cankered branches, cutting back beyond the affected areas, and spray the entire tree with copper-based fungicide in August and again in September.

## Botrytis

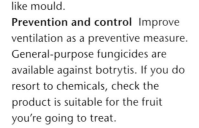

Grey mould, also known as botrytis, is a common problem in greenhouses and also polytunnels, especially early in the year when conditions are cold, dull and damp, and where ventilation is poor. It can affect leaves, flowers and fruit, which will become covered with a grey, felt-like mould.

**Prevention and control** Improve ventilation as a preventive measure. General-purpose fungicides are available against botrytis. If you do resort to chemicals, check the product is suitable for the fruit you're going to treat.

## Brown rot

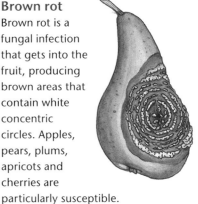

Brown rot is a fungal infection that gets into the fruit, producing brown areas that contain white concentric circles. Apples, pears, plums, apricots and cherries are particularly susceptible.

**Prevention and control** Pick off and burn affected fruit. Practise good cultivation techniques, as the rot gets in through damage caused by pests.

## Fireblight

Fireblight is a bacterial disease that blackens flowers, leaves and shoots, which wilt as if they have been burnt. Oozing cankers may be found on infected stems when the flowers appear.

This disease affects apples, pears, quinces and other members of the rose family, such as hawthorn (*Crataegus*), cotoneaster and flowering quince (*Chaenomeles*).

**Prevention and control** There is no cure; remove affected branches, taking a good margin of healthy growth too – 30cm (1ft) in small branches, 60cm (2ft) in larger ones. Destroy these prunings. Make sure you disinfect your pruning tools.

## Leaf spots

Blackcurrants, gooseberries, medlars and quinces are all vulnerable to leaf spot diseases, which are caused by fungal infection. Although they're rarely a serious threat, they can affect the overall health of your plants, and so their yields.

**Prevention and control** Clear up and burn the diseased leaves at the end of the growing season. Mulch the soil well to prevent spores being splashed up onto the plants. Spray with a copper-based fungicide as a preventive measure.

## Powdery mildew

This is a fungal disease that manifests itself on the leaves, which appear to be covered with white powder. The foliage also turns yellow and may appear thin-textured and deformed.

**Prevention and control** Avoid overcrowding your plants to ensure that air can circulate freely around them. Water and mulch all fruit plants well, because mildew is frequently a sign that the soil is too dry around the roots. Remove affected leaves if possible.

## Silver leaf

Leaves of trees (particularly plums and cherries) adopt a silvery sheen, then they turn brown and die. Brownish-purple brackets appear on stems. To make a diagnosis, cut an affected stem and look at the cut end – a brown stain running down the centre will confirm the cause.

**Prevention and control** Prune in summer, when there are few fungal spores in the air. If silver leaf has already taken hold, cut out affected shoots 15cm (6in) or more past the point where the central core is stained. Pruning paints used to be recommended but aren't nowadays.

## Viruses

There are many viral diseases, most of which reveal themselves in blotching, marbling or yellowing of the foliage; the leaves may also be distorted or grouped in rosettes. Viruses affect the vigour of the plant and so its ability to crop well. Cucumber mosaic virus is a particular problem of passionfruit (*see* page 102).

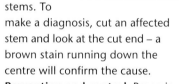

**Prevention and control** There are no cures. Destroy affected plants and keep greenfly under control to prevent viruses spreading. Also, buy healthy, virus-free plants in the first place. Control potential carriers (insect pests) and clear away weeds, which may harbour viruses. Remove and burn affected plants and do not propagate from them.

## Low yields

Low yields are disappointing, especially if you don't know the cause. They may be due to:

■ Lack of a pollinating partner nearby (*see* box, page 19).

■ Cold weather preventing pollinating insects from visiting your plants and frosts killing off flowers before they are pollinated (*see* page 46).

■ Birds getting to your fruit before you do (*see* pages 46–7).

■ A dry spell as the fruit are developing, leading to fruit drop.

■ Poor cultivation techniques – fruit plants work hard and need plenty of food and water (*see* pages 38–9).

■ Plants struggling in unsuitable conditions (refer to the A–Z directory for the likes and dislikes of your particular plant, *see* pages 74–115).

■ A heavy crop the previous year – allowing your tree to carry a full crop can mean a year without fruit. Thin fruit, particularly plums (*see* page 73).

■ Too much lush growth – avoid giving your plants too much nitrogen.

■ Too much or too little pruning (*see* pruning advice on pages 54–73).

# Pruning

If you're going to grow fruit successfully, pruning is a necessity. It will keep plants healthy and yield a better crop of fruit as a result. The only fruits that you won't need to prune are strawberries and rhubarb, although even they need a bit of a tidy up occasionally. Pruning isn't difficult – despite what many people might think – but you do need to set time aside and be systematic in your approach.

# Why prune?

It's a bit of a cliché, but pruning really is like paying a visit to the hairdresser. Most fruit plants could, in theory, be allowed to grow as they like and they would survive and bear a crop of sorts. However, to crop well and produce good-looking fruit of a decent size, they need to be actively maintained and controlled, and this is done by pruning.

Whatever plants you're growing, there are four main reasons to prune: to improve shape; to restrict or reduce growth; to train growth; and for health (that is, to remove dead, diseased or damaged wood that could cause problems if left alone, *see* box, right). Each of these needs to be considered every time you prune fruit plants, but with the additional consideration that they're also done in a way that will improve cropping. Depending on the type of fruit, some plants need pruning only if absolutely necessary, while others need pruning once, twice or even three times a year.

Apples are pruned in winter and summer. Winter pruning of trained trees (shown here) concentrates on thinning out the fruiting stems, or spurs, to ensure that there is enough space for the crop to grow. The aim of summer pruning is to remove unproductive new growth. (*See also* pages 64 and 76–8.)

## Pruning for larger crops

A plant should grow in balance with its roots, so the bigger the plant, the more extensive its root system. When you prune, you reduce the number of branches or amount of top-growth on the plant, in effect reducing the roots' workload. This has the effect of concentrating the plant's energy and, in the case of fruit-bearing plants, the result is larger fruit or a bigger crop. But that is not the end of the story. With fruit you also select those branches that are most capable of bearing fruit, and then you encourage them to produce as much as possible.

When they've finished fruiting, autumn-fruiting raspberry canes are cut right back down to the ground. This encourages the growth of new stems that will fruit next year.

## Pruning for health

When trees and shrubs are allowed to grow naturally without human interference, they will produce branches that may be crooked, densely packed or grow across each other. Even if they develop perfectly neatly, some will be damaged by outside forces, such as the weather, insects or animals.

When you prune for health, you look for this type of branch and either cut it back or cut it off altogether. This way, you prevent disease getting into the plant through damaged bark, create space for the remaining branches to grow freely, and remove weak branches that might split or break off, which can cause serious damage to the whole plant. In short, you maintain a plant's vigour.

## Don't forget

If you buy a poorly shaped, weak specimen, it will take years of careful pruning to make improvements. It's vital to purchase something that looks good and healthy in the first place.

# Tools and equipment

There's a wide variety of pruning tools, and it's well worth getting the very best quality you can afford, so that when you prune you feel as if you're practising an art – which you are – rather than completing a chore. As well as the satisfaction you'll get from using comfortable, well-made equipment, there's the benefit of having fine, sharp blades that will ensure you make good, clean and tidy cuts every time.

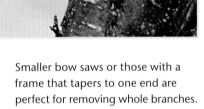

## Secateurs

Secateurs are the mainstay of any pruning tool collection. They can cope with woody shoots up to about 1cm (½in) thick. There are two main types of secateur: anvil and bypass. Anvil secateurs work a bit like a guillotine and have one sharp blade that closes down onto a flat edge. Bypass secateurs (*see* opposite) are like scissors, with two blades that cut as they pass each other. There is little to choose between the two, except bypass secateurs are better for cutting brittle or hollow stems.

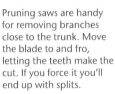

Pruning saws are handy for removing branches close to the trunk. Move the blade to and fro, letting the teeth make the cut. If you force it you'll end up with splits.

## Pruning saw

There are several types of pruning saw; all are intended to cut branches that are too big for secateurs.

The teeth of single-edged saws cut on the backwards, or 'pull', stroke; the blade may be straight or slightly curved. Choose one with a blade that tapers to a point, as this will make it easier to use in tight spaces.

Double-edged saws have coarse teeth on one side and small, fine teeth on the other; both cut on the 'pull' stroke. The coarse edge is ideal for living, sappy wood, while the fine edge is better on dead, dry wood.

Bow saws have a blade fitted to a sprung, bow-shaped frame. The blade has coarse teeth that cut on the forwards, or 'push', stroke.

Smaller bow saws or those with a frame that tapers to one end are perfect for removing whole branches.

## Loppers

Long-handled pruners, or loppers, are industrial-strength secateurs on long handles, which increase the leverage, enabling you to cut more using less muscle power. Some have extendable handles, giving even more leverage and more reach. Again, they may have an anvil or bypass cutting action. If you have a very tall tree to contend with, you might need long-arm loppers, which are basically the same thing as ordinary loppers but on the end of a very long pole.

## Gardening knife

All gardeners really must have a gardening or pruning knife. These indispensable multipurpose tools can be used for tweaking off green shoots, taking cuttings, slicing string and tidying pruning cuts.

Long-handled loppers are ideal for those out-of-reach places. To cut thick branches, choose a pair with a ratchet; if you need to do a lot of cutting, a gear action takes the effort out of the job.

# How to prune

Pruning is one of those things that you get better at with practice. Fortunately, plants are quite forgiving and can recover from minor mistakes; even so, it's important to follow a few tried and tested rules and to do your utmost to get it right, as you'll be reminded of your errors as often as you look at the plant. If in doubt, follow the old carpenter's law: measure twice (in the case of pruning, consider twice), cut once.

## Using your tools

The basic rule for using pruning tools is to look at the thickness of the stem or branch to be cut and to choose a tool capable of cutting it with ease. For stems up to 1cm (½in) thick, secateurs are best, as they're easily manipulated into small spaces and will make a good, clean cut. For stems 1–2.5cm (½–1in) thick, choose loppers. Anything thicker, and you'll need a pruning saw (*see* opposite).

If you start to try to make a cut with your secateurs and it's clear they'll find the job difficult, don't persist – get out your larger tools. If you force cuts, you'll end up with ragged edges and damaged secateurs. Position the stem centrally between the blades, not at the tip, and don't be tempted to twist them to finish the cut.

## Where and how to cut

The basic rule for where to cut is near a bud; to be precise about 6mm (¼in) beyond the bud, so it

sits right at the new end of the stem. The reason for cutting to a healthy bud is that this is where growth hormones are concentrated and these encourage healing as well as growth. If you cut, say, midway between two buds, you're cutting into a 'no-man's-land' where less growth takes place, and there's a far greater risk of disease entering the wound, because it will take much longer to heal.

When you cut at a bud, it will grow away in the direction it was pointing and form a new stem. Imagine you have a nice straight stem that is too long. First, decide how long you want the stem to be, then find a bud a few centimetres short of this position (otherwise, the new growth resulting from your pruning will instantly be too long).

## Jargon busting

Pruning can seem daunting enough without having to understand the terms used to describe plant anatomy. However, once you know what they refer to these terms do make the job clearer.

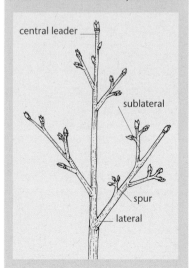

central leader

sublateral

spur

lateral

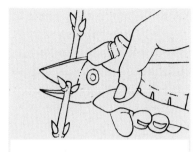

A straight cut above opposite buds.

An angled cut above an alternate bud.

Choose a bud that is facing in the direction you would like the stem to grow – this is normally outwards, away from the centre of the plant, to prevent overcrowding – then make your cut just above it.

## Cutting angles

On plants that produce buds on alternate sides up a stem, make an angled cut (about 25 degrees), sloping the cut away from the bud (*see* above). This is ideal, since the angle prevents water or sap from collecting at the cut surface, which would inhibit healing. However, on plants that produce paired (also known as opposite) buds, you'll need to cut straight across the stem, just above the buds (*see* top). Remember, neat cuts heal more quickly than ragged ones.

# Pruning freestanding fruit trees

Modern fruit trees are easier to grow and maintain than ever before. The dwarf trees that are now available to the home gardener are much easier to pick and prune than their traditional orchard-size cousins, and methods of pruning and training fruit trees have been developed to increase fruit-bearing and to work with the natural growth pattern of the plant. If you have a smallish garden, there are three main ways of growing freestanding fruit trees – as bushes, pyramids or columns. All of these are pruned when young to create their framework (this training stage is known as 'formative pruning' and is often started off by the nursery). Once the tree is established, you'll need to carry out 'routine' pruning to maintain its shape.

## Take your time

Although most pruning mistakes will grow out with time, it makes sense to avoid them in the first place.

■ Allow yourself plenty of time to prune each tree – rushing can result in errors.

■ Decide where to prune, then before cutting, stand back and double-check the effect of the cut you're about to make.

■ If in doubt, leave a branch slightly long; you can always cut it shorter later.

■ Remove dead and crossing branches first, and always make the cut just above a bud to help the healing process.

## Bush-form and half-standard trees

Bush-form fruit trees have a short, clear stem above which are the branches (see pages 12–13). These are pruned to maintain what is called an 'open centre', to help ripening, make picking easier, and to maintain a balance between the formation of new, healthy growth and the production of good-quality fruits. If you have a larger garden and are growing half-standards, the stem or trunk will be longer, but the principles behind the pruning are the same.

Most young trees are given formative pruning in the nursery before being sold, so the bush or half-standard tree you buy should already have a central leader (main stem) without branches for the first 75cm (30in), above which it will have three to four evenly spaced branches (laterals) radiating out.

Pruning can be an enjoyable activity and is a great way of getting out into the garden in the winter, when it's too wet to dig or plant.

## HOW TO create a bush-form tree

**1**

In late autumn or early winter, prune back the central leader to 25cm (10in) above the top lateral, just above a bud. Cut back the laterals by half, just above an outward-facing bud. The laterals will form the basis of the permanent framework.

**2**

In late summer, cut back to three leaves any sublaterals that are not required for future branches – those that are crowded, rubbing against each other, damaged or growing in the wrong direction. Do not prune the laterals or leader.

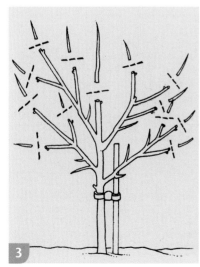

**3**

The following autumn or winter, cut back the leader to 25cm (10in), as in step 1. Prune new branches back by half, and those formed in the previous year by one third of their new growth, always cutting just above an outward-facing bud.

**4**

In late summer the following year, again cut back the sublateral shoots to three leaves, and any shoots emerging from these sublateral shoots to just one leaf. Leave uncut any shoots that are shorter than 20cm (8in).

These laterals will form the basis of the permanent bush shape, which you will create over a period of three to four years after planting, until you have an open framework of about eight to ten laterals, each with several sublaterals (*see* left).

Once this structural framework has been established, only winter pruning is necessary. The extent of winter pruning needed will vary from year to year, depending on the previous season and the type and amount of growth that was made: there is always more pruning to do after a wet growing season. The fruiting habit of the tree will also determine how it is pruned – spur-bearing trees need regular spur-thinning, while tip-bearing ones are pruned using what is known as a renewal technique (*see* pages 76–8).

## Pyramid trees

A pyramid tree is created around a central main stem that has a framework of branches radiating out from it, with the branches becoming progressively shorter towards the top (*see* pages 12–13). The aim is to maximize space between the fruiting branches, allowing light into the tree to aid ripening and to make picking easier. Spindlebushes are a supported and more rigidly trained version of pyramid trees. Spur-bearing fruit trees (*see* page 77) are suitable for growing as pyramids.

Dwarf pyramid trees can be bought part-trained with at least the lower tier of branches already formed, but it's more common to buy a 'feathered maiden'. This is a young tree that has a single central

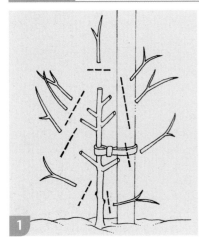

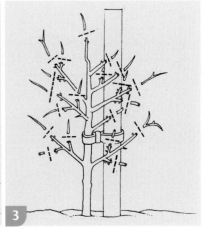

**1** In the first winter after planting, prune back the central leader to a strong, healthy bud about 60–75cm (24–30in) above soil level. Remove any unwanted laterals and prune those that remain to within 15cm (6in) of the main stem.

**2** During the first summer after planting, prune back any new laterals to five leaves. These will mostly be emerging from near the top of the tree and pruning them begins to form the distinctive pyramid tree shape.

**3** After leaf fall in the second winter, cut back all of the current season's growth to leave about 25cm (10in) of the new growth. The aim is to build a sturdy stem and strong framework of branches capable of carrying fruit-bearing spurs.

leader with about five laterals of various lengths.

After planting, or during the first winter, shorten the leader and laterals and remove or trim weak or damaged shoots (*see* above). After this, during the early years of the tree's life, aim to build a sturdy stem and strong framework of well-spaced branches capable of carrying fruit-bearing spurs.

Once the pyramid shape is established, prune twice a year (*see* right). Summer prune to control the vigour of the shoots and direct the tree's energies into developing fruit-bearing growth. Winter prune to control the overall height, size and shape of the tree; any spur-thinning (*see* page 77) is also carried out in winter. Consider root pruning if the tree is becoming too large for its allotted space (*see* page 63).

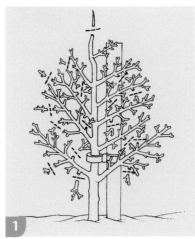

**1** Each winter, after leaf fall, trim off the top of the central leader, leaving about five buds on the current season's growth. Prune out overcrowded fruiting spurs to remove the oldest, least productive shoots. Remove some older branches to create space for new shoots to emerge.

**2** In the second and subsequent summers, prune back the new lateral growths to five leaves; prune back any sublaterals to three leaves. (Include tiers formed in previous seasons, as well as the new tier of branches that has formed during the growing season.)

## Columnar trees

The most commonly grown column-shaped fruit trees are the varieties known as minarette or ballerina, which are sold already pruned into a narrow columnar shape. Since these are supplied already pruned, most (if not all) of the formative pruning will already have been carried out. Such a tree will continue to grow as a single column until it reaches about 2–2.5m (6–8ft) high, depending on the variety and the vigour of its rootstock (*see* page 15).

Usually, once the tree starts to crop regularly, little formative pruning is required. However, a certain amount of maintenance pruning will be necessary during summer to make sure it retains its size and shape, to control the shoot growth and to encourage the formation of fruit buds; some pruning in late spring may also be necessary.

### Encouraging sideshoots

One of the main reasons why fruit gardeners have to prune is something called 'apical dominance'. This is when the bud at the very top of a stem produces a hormone that prevents the buds below it from developing into sideshoots. This means that the plant tends to produce mostly long, slender, unbranched stems. In most cases, branching is preferable as the more branches you have, the more opportunities there are for flowers to form, and thus the more fruit you will get. Removing the bud at the end of the stem allows the sideshoots to develop. (A major exception is with ballerina fruit trees, where apical dominance has been exploited to produce a plant that is very narrow in comparison with its height.)

Apical dominance can also be broken by training the stems of plants horizontally (*see* Fan-trained and espaliers, pages 14 and 65–8). Each bud on the top side of a horizontal stem is then able to develop and produce flowering and then fruiting buds, rather than just the end one.

## HOW TO maintain an established columnar tree

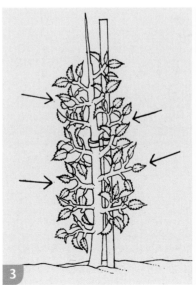

**1**

Each spring and summer allow the central leader to make about 45cm (18in) of new growth, then prune it back to 30cm (12in). In midsummer, once the laterals have produced lots of growth, cut them back to six leaves.

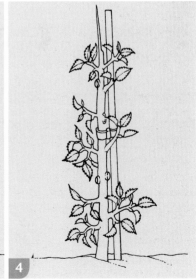

**2**

In mid- or late summer, check the new growth on the leader and prune it back again if necessary. Once the sublaterals have grown to about 15cm (6in) long, cut them back to a single leaf. This produces the branching fruit-bearing structures, or spurs.

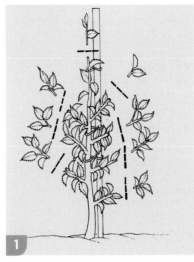

**3**

In late spring, remove some spurs to prevent overcrowding and remove any sucker growths or emerging laterals that may form at the base of the tree.

**4**

Ideally, you'll remove up to one third of the spurs. The aim is to grow a tree that has short fruit-bearing spurs, which will encourage good-sized fruits.

# Bark ringing fruit trees

If your fruit trees are growing too vigorously and not fruiting as well as you think they should, consider using a pruning technique called bark ringing. It is suitable for apples and pears, but must never be used on stone fruit, such as plums or cherries, as it will make them very vulnerable to silver leaf disease.

Bark ringing involves removing a strip of bark from around the trunk, thereby restricting the flow of sap (and nutrients) to the top of the tree and limiting the supply of foodstuffs to the roots. Although it can be very successful, it should be performed only once a year and must be done with great care, as making a cut like this provides fungal or bacterial disease with a great opportunity to enter the plant, which could be fatal.

The aim is to remove a narrow strip (ring) of bark from around the stem of the tree, exposing the wood beneath in late spring when the tree is in full growth. The ring should be wide enough to restrict sap flow, but not so wide that it's unable to heal within a year. (A longer healing time may result in damage to the tree.)

Ideally, make your bark rings about 75cm (30in) above soil level and inspect the cuts regularly to check pests such as woodlice aren't inhibiting healing.

Bark ringing can be repeated every year if required, but you must never remove the bark from exactly the same place twice. Always make any new cuts just above or just below the cuts that you've made in previous years.

Lift the strip of cut bark from around the trunk, taking care not to introduce dirt into the exposed area.

## Don't forget

You will be making deep intrusive cuts into the tree. Make sure your pruning knife is sharp and very clean, like a surgeon's scalpel.

## HOW TO bark ring a fruit tree

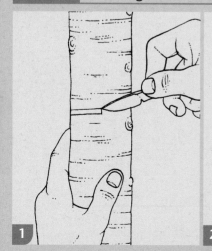

**1** Make two horizontal, parallel cuts, between 3mm (⅛in) and 1cm (½in) apart, depending on the size of the tree, all the way around the stem.

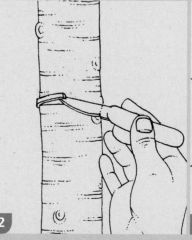

**2** Using the tip of the knife, start to lift the bark out from between the two cuts. Pull this strip of bark away from the tree to leave a clear 'ring' of bark-free trunk.

**3** Once all the bark has been removed, protect the open wound with a strip of electrician's insulation tape, stuck to the bark on either side of the cut, not the inner tissue.

# Root pruning fruit trees

Root pruning is a way of checking the growth of fruit trees that are growing vigorously at the expense of cropping. By removing some of the tree's root system you're putting the tree under stress, so it will try to reproduce itself before its demise. As a result, your fruit yields should improve within a couple of years.

Root pruning should be carried out only in winter, when the tree is dormant. And it should not be undertaken too often. However, once the tree has fully recovered and new, strong roots begin to grow again (evident from vigorous shoot growth), the desired effects of the root prune will dwindle and the operation may have to be repeated.

With trees that are less than five years old, the best way to root prune is to dig up the tree, cleanly cut away any large roots with a pruning saw or secateurs (leaving as many of the fine, fibrous roots as possible), and then replant. Take care not to allow the fibrous roots to dry out before replanting in the same (or new, more desirable) position. Always replant the tree at the depth it was set at originally.

Trees that are more than five years old are likely to be too large to dig up and replant, so the operation must be carried out *in situ* by exposing a section of the root system 1.2–1.5m (4–5ft) from the trunk, and cutting the larger, thicker roots back (*see* below). Very mature trees can be treated in the same way, except the process should be spread over two or three winters and the trench should be dug just outside the diameter of the tree's leaf canopy, or it will be too much of a shock to the tree's system.

After any root-pruning operation, enrich the soil with well-rotted manure or garden compost and stake the tree to give it support (*see* page 28). Water well in dry weather, too.

If, after root pruning, a tree continues to put on too much growth, it is likely that the rootstock (*see* page 15) is too vigorous for the situation; the only solution then is to replace the tree.

## Don't forget

When you prune the roots of a tree, you effectively remove its anchors. This, of course, affects its stability, so always provide additional support, such as a stake, after root pruning.

## HOW TO root prune a fruit tree

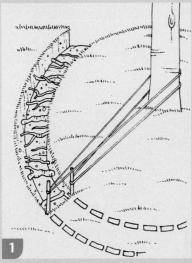

**1** Using pegs and garden twine, measure out and then dig a trench around the tree. The inner edge of the trench should be 1.2–1.5m (4–5ft) from the trunk, depending on the size of the tree. Make the trench 30–40cm (12–16in) deep.

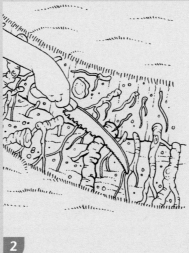

**2** Having exposed a section of the root system, cut through and dispose of all the large, thick roots using a pruning saw or loppers. Try to avoid damaging the finer fibrous roots in the process if at all possible.

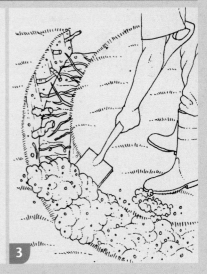

**3** Spread out any remaining fibrous roots in the trench. Refill the trench with the excavated soil, enriching it as you go with well-rotted manure or good garden compost, and adding a stake if necessary (*see* page 28). Firm the soil and water well.

# Pruning supported trees

Dwarfing rootstocks have led to the development of a number of ways of growing fruit trees along wires. Known as supported or trained trees, these have the advantage of fitting into very little space, and if the wires are against a wall or fence, they have protection against the worst of the weather. Like the small freestanding fruit trees, their size makes them easy to harvest and prune. Supported trees include cordons, espaliers and fans.

### Creating a stepover

Apples on a dwarf rootstock can be trained at a very low height to create a stepover (*see* pages 14 and 21). After planting or in winter, reduce the laterals (sideshoots) to three or four buds. Don't prune the leader. In subsequent winters, thin the spurs if necessary and remove the tip of the leader.

## Cordons

A cordon is basically a 'pole' of growth that produces fruit on short, twiggy spurs that emerge along its length. Cordons can be upright or at a 45-degree angle supported on canes or wires. They can be planted individually or several can be positioned 45cm (18in) apart to form a 'hedge' (*see* pages 13–14).

Cordons can be bought already trained or you can do the formative pruning yourself (*see* opposite). You will need a 'feathered maiden', which is a young tree with a leader (main stem) and several laterals (sideshoots). For an angled cordon, plant the feathered maiden at a slant and tie it to a cane which itself is attached to a framework of wires (*see* pages 30–1). To form and then maintain the cordon, cut out the tip of the leader in midsummer every year, keeping it to a height

### Don't forget

Training is an intensive method of fruit production and as a result the trees tend to be shorter-lived than freestanding ones.

Summer pruning of trained apple trees, such as cordons, is aimed at removing some of the new growth, which is not needed for healthy cropping.

convenient for maintenance and harvesting. Also in summer, cut back new shoots, reducing each new lateral to three leaves – these will form the fruiting spurs – and sublaterals (shoots growing off the sideshoots) to one leaf. Each summer, repeat this pruning, cutting back the current year's growth on laterals to three leaves and that on sublaterals to one leaf.

## Espaliers

An espalier is created by training a tree into a series of two or more tiers of horizontal branches, which has the effect of increasing the yield of fruit (*see* pages 14 and 66). The branches are about 40cm (16in) apart and trained in opposite pairs at right angles to the main stem. Espalier trees are usually sold part-trained, with at least one completed pair of horizontal branches, but

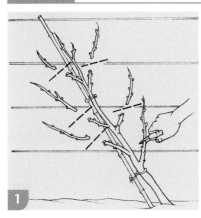

**1** After planting or in the first winter, prune laterals over 10cm (4in) to four buds; cut just above an outward-facing bud.

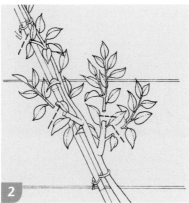

**2** The following summer, prune new growth to three leaves. Prune sublaterals to one leaf. This creates the fruiting spur.

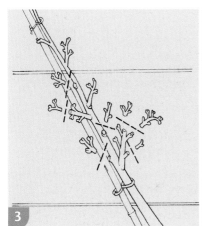

**3** In subsequent winters, thin crowded fruiting spurs (*see* page 77). When the leader reaches the top wire, trim the new growth back to one leaf in late spring.

**4** Every summer, prune new laterals to three leaves and sublaterals to one leaf. Reduce new growth on mature laterals to three leaves and sublaterals to one leaf.

A well-trained espalier such as this pear is both decorative and productive, creating an attractive focal point on a wall or fence when in flower and when bearing fruit.

### What did I do wrong?

The aim of pruning is to achieve the right balance between fruiting, the production of new growth, and achieving the correct shape. If your plants are producing a huge amount of new growth but (later in the season) very little fruit, it's likely you were somewhat overzealous with the secateurs. If they produce hardly any new growth at all, you were probably not assertive enough to spur the plant into growth – you might get plenty of fruit this year but there won't be enough new growth to produce a good crop next year. Don't be disheartened, a little practice is all that is needed.

often with two, and a third partially formed.

Initial training concentrates on producing the framework of horizontal branches. Each year the central leader is pruned back to the nearest horizontal wire, ideally where three healthy buds are located close together; two of these form the next tier of branches and the third makes the new main stem, which will be trained vertically as it grows. As they grow, the two shoots that will form the next tier of branches are trained onto canes set at a 45-degree angle; these are bent down to horizontal at the end of the growing season. The process is repeated annually until the desired number of tiers has been achieved. Once the espalier has filled the space allotted to it, simply remove all the current season's extension growth each winter.

## HOW TO create and maintain an espalier

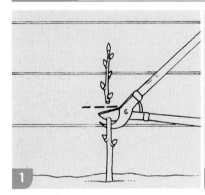

**1** Start with an unbranched stem or 'maiden whip'. In the first winter, shorten it to just above a wire at about 45cm (18in) above ground level. As new growth begins, select two strong shoots to form the first laterals of the espalier.

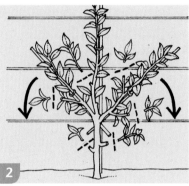

**2** In summer, start training the shoots on canes set at 45 degrees. Cut back to five buds any shoots that grow from them. Remove unwanted shoots from the main stem. At the end of summer, lower the laterals and tie them to the wires.

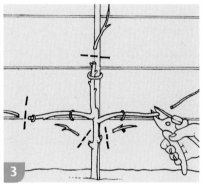

**3** The following winter, cut back the central leader to the wire immediately above the new tier of branches. Prune the horizontally growing branches back by one third to create a strong framework and encourage fruit-bearing spurs.

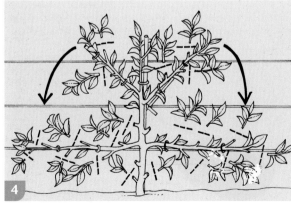

**4** The following summer, select another two shoots to form the next tier. Tie them to canes and prune and lower them as in the first summer. Repeat this each year until you have the number of branches you want, then remove the leader in summer.

**5** Each midsummer, as the bases of the new sublaterals from the branch framework become woody, prune them back to three buds. Prune weak growth back to a single bud. In winter, thin out the spur systems (see page 77).

## Fan-trained trees

Many of the stone fruits, such as apricots, cherries, peaches and some varieties of plum, as well as almonds and figs, will not grow or fruit well if exposed to cold or windy weather. Fan-training is a way of growing these trees against a wall or fence, which takes advantage of the residual heat provided by the background support structure and provides shelter from the worst of the weather (*see* pages 13–14).

This tree form is created by training a series of laterals and sublaterals that radiate out in an arc from a short leg, or stem. Training the shoots at an angle reduces apical dominance and so encourages branching (*see* page 61). Fans can be bought part-trained or you can form one yourself using a feathered maiden. The process normally takes three to four years. A structural

## HOW TO create a fan-trained tree

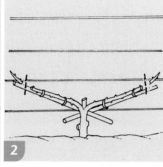

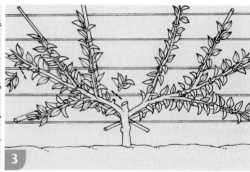

**1** In the first year after planting, remove all but two shoots at a height of about 30cm (12in) above the ground. Train these to the right and left, tying them onto the support frame. These will form the framework branches.

**2** In late winter, cut back the two laterals, or ribs, to an upward-facing bud emerging about 45cm (18in) from the main stem. This will encourage sublaterals to form and create a strong base for the fan.

**3** Throughout the second summer after the initial training, tie in the extension growth from the branches, and allow two or three suitably spaced sublaterals to grow on each branch. Tie these to canes, and prune out or cut back to one bud any competing shoots as they grow. By removing these shoots you'll allow the others to grow stronger.

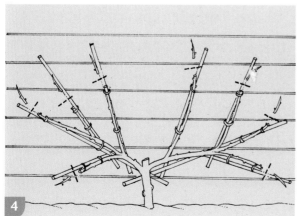

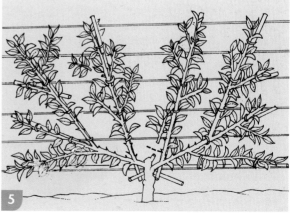

**4** In the third spring, prune the end third of each branch, leaving mature wood from the previous season. The shortening of the branches will encourage fruiting spurs to develop.

**5** In the third summer, allow two or three suitably spaced branches to grow from each sideshoot, tying them to canes. Repeat this until a well-branched fan fills the available space.

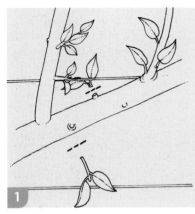

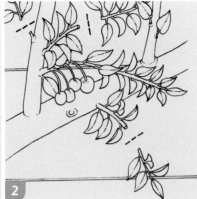

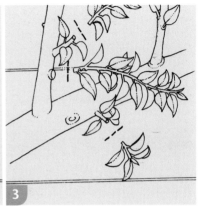

**1** In late spring, remove any buds that are growing directly into the support structure or out at right angles from the fan structure and its support.

**2** In midsummer, select one or two shoots to replace each of this year's fruit-bearing shoots. Cut each of these shoots back to six leaves.

**3** In late summer, remove the shoots that fruited this year. Trim the selected replacement shoots back again to three leaves to encourage fruit buds to form.

support of horizontal wires (*see* pages 30–1) and canes (*see* right) is used to shape and hold the fan in place.

In the early stages, formative pruning (*see* page 67) involves training shoots of similar size, which are spread out evenly to form a framework of shoots – the 'ribs' of the fan. Later, pruning focuses on creating fruiting buds: the ribs are allowed to extend and are tied into the support frame. Smaller branches (sublaterals) growing from these ribs are the shoots that will carry the following year's blossom.

With routine pruning (*see* above), the aim is to provide a constant supply of young shoots to replace the old wood. This is usually done after harvesting the fruits: the fruiting shoot is pruned out, to be replaced with a shoot that is emerging just below where the cut was made. Pruning must be carried out regularly for fan-trained trees.

This plum is well on its way to being a fully trained fan. The well-prepared gardener has already put in place suitable supports for the final branches.

# Pruning soft fruit

As with tree fruit, the aim of pruning soft fruit is to produce a good crop while keeping the plants healthy. With spiny soft fruit there's the added challenge of keeping the fruit accessible, and with those that grow very vigorously pruning is a necessity, just to be able to get around them in the garden. Although the pruning and training regime must be strict and regular, it is reasonably straightforward if you follow a few simple rules.

## Cane fruit

This group includes raspberries, blackberries and a host of plants that are either related to blackberries or very similar to them. They produce their crops on what are best described as many-stemmed, shapeless plants. The stems may be thorny and are either long and trailing or shorter and more erect. The plants are shapeless because they can grow and spread in any direction by underground suckers or by producing roots where the stems touch the ground. These plants usually bear fruit prodigiously whether or not they're pruned, but they're mostly very unruly and need

### Standard and half-standard gooseberries

Gooseberries grown as standards or half-standards (see page 50) are the same varieties as those grown as bushes, but they've been grafted onto a rootstock with a longer leg: about 1.2m (4ft) for a standard, 60–90cm (2–3ft) for a half-standard. Standards and half-standards must be staked (see page 28), as the stem isn't strong enough to support the weight of the cropping cultivar. Prune these plants in exactly the same way and at the same time as the bush forms (see page 70), and remove any sucker growths that emerge from the rootstock as soon as they appear.

Raspberries are traditionally trained and supported on a system of wires; their pruning is uncomplicated and involves cutting out whole canes.

to be kept under control in your garden, otherwise they'll take over and become a nuisance. Also the older stems gradually become less productive so should be removed on a regular basis. With cane fruit it's vital to provide suitable support such as wires (see pages 30–1) and frequently tie in the stems.

For the purposes of pruning, cane fruits are divided into two main groups. Group 1 contains the plants that have upright, stiff, erect growth. These are mostly the raspberries, but also some forms of blackberry that are specifically bred

to be fairly upright and only semi-trailing. Group 2 contains the plants that have a lax habit, producing long, trailing stems. These are most of the blackberries, as well as boysenberries, loganberries and tayberries. Group 1 is divided again into summer-fruiting raspberries and autumn-fruiting raspberries, which need slightly different treatment. This all sounds a little complicated, but in fact the pruning of cane fruit is not difficult as long as it's carried out when necessary, and combined with a careful and regular tying-in routine.

The pruning of group 1 cane fruits is covered under raspberries (see pages 110–11). The pruning of group 2 cane fruits is covered under blackberries (see pages 80–1).

## Bush fruit

Bush fruits include gooseberries, redcurrants, whitecurrants and blackcurrants. With the exception of blackcurrants (see pages 82–3), these are usually grown as freestanding plants on a short stem (known as a leg), or as standards or half-standards to keep the fruit above the ground (especially useful for plants that have a lax, weeping habit, such as many gooseberries). You can grow bush fruit as cordons (see pages 13–14 and 64), but this is a tricky method that isn't worth the trouble unless space is very limited.

Gooseberries, redcurrants and whitecurrants produce fruits on short spurs, which are developed by pruning back the laterals. Most of the fruits are produced on laterals that are two or three years old; those that are four or more years old produce very few.

The best time to carry out formative pruning is late winter or early spring, before growth begins (see step 1, left). In subsequent years, aim to create and maintain a wine-glass shape. The idea is to keep the centre of the bush reasonably open. This helps the fruits to ripen, makes picking easier, and improves air circulation (see step 2, left).

A properly pruned, established plant should consist of nine to twelve laterals, ranging from one to three years of age. All four-year-old laterals should be removed.

---

**HOW TO** prune bush fruit with a 'leg'

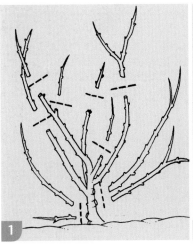

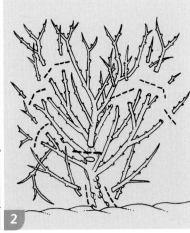

In the first winter (or immediately after planting), remove laterals lower than 20cm (8in) above ground level to form the 'leg' of the bush. Select up to six healthy, undamaged laterals to form a framework, and prune these back to half their original length, cutting above an outward-facing bud. Remove all other laterals. The next winter, cut back all the new growth by half. Prune back to a single bud any shoots growing into the centre of the bush or in a downward direction so fruit-bearing spurs develop.

In late winter or early spring of subsequent years, remove any dead, damaged, diseased, weak or low-growing shoots. Reduce overcrowded or crossing stems to about 2cm (¾in) long. Cut out old, unproductive laterals, and shorten the rest by about a quarter. Later, prune out all four-year-old laterals, thinning out some of the new growth. Cut out any old, non-fruiting shoots to encourage strong young shoots to grow. Cut back the sublaterals to the length of a finger in summer to form fruiting spurs.

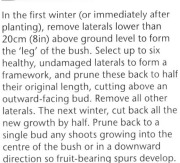

# Pruning vines

Vines tend to be very vigorous, fast- and strong-growing plants, with very little natural shape. Left to their own devices they would literally run rampant – along the ground, over pergolas, up arches and into trees. The grape is still the most commonly grown vine, but has now been joined by kiwis and passionfruit, both of which can produce fruit outside in a warm, sheltered position and benefit from careful control and training.

For gardeners it is most practical to grow vines as climbers on a wall or fence, particularly where space is limited. The most common pruning techniques are the cordon (or rod-and-spur) method, which involves having a semi-permanent framework, and the renewal

## HOW TO train a cordon vine up and across a pergola (rod-and-spur method)

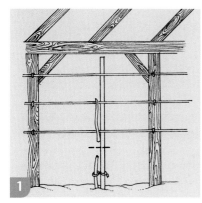

**1**

Plant the vine at the pergola base in late autumn or early winter, then shorten the rod (stem) by two thirds, cutting just above a bud. This will encourage the vine to establish a strong root system.

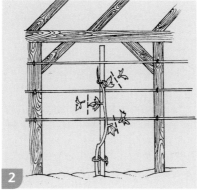

**2**

During the growing season, select one strong shoot to continue as the rod, and train it vertically on a cane. Remove any tendrils and cut any sideshoots (spurs) emerging from it to one leaf.

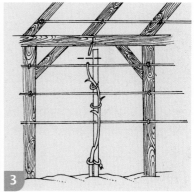

**3**

In winter, prune back the rod to a strong, healthy bud, as near as possible to the overhead training support. Fix wires on the overhead supports, ready for training the vine horizontally next year.

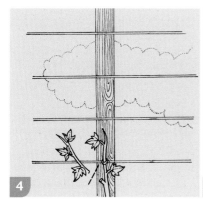

**4**

(Overhead horizontal support of pergola, viewed from below.) As new growth begins in spring, select one strong shoot to be the horizontal rod and tie it in to prevent it being damaged by the wind.

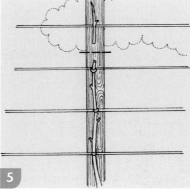

**5**

(Viewed from below.) As the selected rod grows, continue to tie it in horizontally along the support structure. In late autumn or early winter, cut back the end third of the horizontal rod.

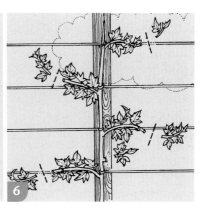

**6**

(Viewed from below.) Allow strong spurs to develop every 30cm (12in). Cut these to five or six leaves in summer. Remove surplus shoots, allowing those that form on the vertical rod to retain one leaf.

method, in which the framework is replaced (renewed) over one to three years. Growing a grapevine over a pergola using the cordon method is covered here; for other methods, *see* pages 92–4 (grapes), 95–6 (kiwi fruit) and 102 (passionfruit).

## Growing a cordon grape

With the cordon method, you create a framework on which permanent fruiting spurs are formed. Spurs develop from buds that break at intervals along the rod (main stem). There may be a single rod or two. The rods can be trained vertically or horizontally – or both (for example, vertically up the wall of a house, then horizontally over a structure such as a pergola or along the wall).

Grapevines produce fruit on the current season's growth, which means that spring and summer

A grapevine creates wonderful dappled shade when grown over a pergola. It will not fruit heavily if left to its own devices, but simple cordon pruning (*see* page 71 and below) should provide you with a few bunches to enjoy in a good summer.

pruning is necessary to limit the number of flower trusses that form and mature in each spur system. Pruning also restricts the growth of the sideshoots, ensuring that the foliage canopy does not prevent light from getting to the fruit and hinder ripening.

During formative pruning, train one stem up to at least 2m (6ft) so that the grapes will hang above head height; on a house wall, you may need to train it above the height of ground-floor windows. Once the required height has been reached, train the main stem horizontally until it reaches the desired length; this growth will form the permanent framework; the fruit-bearing spurs are trained at right angles to the main horizontal stem on an annual basis.

Once a fruiting framework has been created, allow each spur to produce two laterals. In each case, let the stronger lateral shoot grow; it will carry the grapes later. Pinch back the weaker shoots to two leaves. Over the summer the laterals will produce sublaterals – prune all these back to a single leaf as soon as they appear. When the flower trusses develop, keep only one per lateral. Cut off the laterals two leaves beyond each selected truss. Prune any non-flowering laterals to five or six leaves, and cut back sublaterals to a single leaf.

## HOW TO maintain a cordon vine

(Overhead horizontal support, viewed from below.)

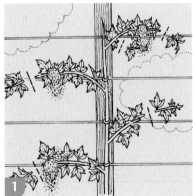

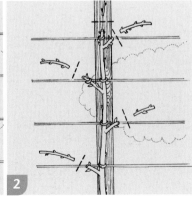

Each spring, allow one spur to form every 30cm (12in). Prune these to two leaves beyond the flower cluster, and any sideshoots to one leaf. Prune non-flowering spurs back to five or six leaves through the summer.

In winter, cut back the spurs to two strong buds. Reduce the new growth on the leader by half until it is the desired length, and from then on cut it back to two buds each winter. These buds will produce the grape-bearing shoots.

# Fruit pruning and thinning timetable

After planting, it takes a couple of years to prune fruit trees into the form required. After this, prune regularly to keep this shape and ensure good yields. Most maintenance pruning is done in winter, but to avoid silver leaf disease the cherry family (apricots, cherries, peaches, nectarines and plums) must be pruned in spring, or better still summer. Fruit thinning is often necessary to produce a healthy crop of good-sized fruit, especially in plants that are still establishing or those with weak or damaged branches. Thinning is best done in stages. Early in the season, remove damaged or poorly shaped fruit using scissors. The second thinning is usually in midsummer, when the fruits are beginning to increase in size and it will be obvious where crowding is occurring.

| FRUIT | PRUNING | THINNING |
| --- | --- | --- |
| **Apples** | Freestanding trees – Winter to early spring (see pages 76–8)<br>Trained trees – Winter to early spring and midsummer | Thin twice: in early June to remove misshapen fruit; then in July to 10–15cm (4–6in) apart for eaters, 15–23cm (6–9in) for cookers, leaving one or two fruit per cluster. |
| **Apricots** | Freestanding trees – Spring or summer (if necessary)<br>Trained trees – Spring and midsummer | Thin gradually to 8–10cm (3–4in) apart, from when they are cherry-sized. |
| **Blackberries and their hybrids** | Spring and late summer to early autumn (see pages 80–1) | Not needed |
| **Blackcurrants** | Winter (see pages 82–3) | Not needed |
| **Blueberries** | Winter | Not needed |
| **Cherries** | Freestanding trees – Spring or summer (if necessary)<br>Trained trees – Spring and midsummer | Not needed |
| **Citrus fruit** | Spring or little and often | Not needed |
| **Cranberries** | Spring (if necessary; no regular pruning required) | Not needed |
| **Figs** | Late winter or early spring and summer (see pages 89–90) | Not needed |
| **Gooseberries** | Winter and summer | For large dessert fruit, remove every other gooseberry from late May. These can be used in cooking. |
| **Grapes** | Indoor grapes – Late autumn to midwinter, spring and summer, depending on technique (see page 93)<br>Informal outdoor grapes – Midwinter<br>Trained outdoor grapes – Late autumn to midwinter, spring and summer, depending on technique (see pages 71–2, 92–4) | Thin bunches once or twice as the fruit swell, snipping off fruit with fine-bladed scissors. |
| **Kiwi fruit** | Midwinter and summer (see pages 95–6) | Not needed |
| **Melons** | Pinch off stem-tips in midsummer | Retain four fruit per plant, one on each of four shoots. |
| **Mulberries** | Freestanding trees – Winter (if necessary)<br>Trained trees – Winter to early spring and midsummer | Not needed |
| **Nectarines** | Freestanding trees – Spring or summer<br>Trained trees – Spring and midsummer | Thin to 15cm (6in) apart gradually from when they are fingertip-sized to when they are walnut-sized. |
| **Nuts** | Almonds – Freestanding spring, trained spring and midsummer<br>Cobnuts and filberts – Late winter (if desired)<br>Chestnuts – Only if necessary<br>Hazelnuts – Only if coppicing, then in winter every three years<br>Walnuts – Only if necessary | Not needed |
| **Passionfruit** | Late winter | Not needed |
| **Peaches** | Freestanding trees – Spring or summer<br>Trained trees – Spring and midsummer | Thin to 23cm (9in) apart gradually from when they are fingertip-sized to when they are walnut-sized. |
| **Pears** | Freestanding trees – Winter to early spring<br>Trained trees – Winter to early spring and midsummer | Thin as apples, but leave two fruit per cluster, 8–10cm (3–4in) apart. |
| **Plums** | Freestanding trees – Spring or summer (if necessary)<br>Trained trees – Spring and midsummer | Thin twice: once when they are the size of your thumb top; and again when they are double this size, to 5–8cm (2–3in) apart. |
| **Quinces and medlars** | Winter if necessary | Not needed |
| **Raspberries** | Summer-fruiting canes – Late summer (see page 110)<br>Autumn-fruiting canes – Late winter and early summer (see page 110–11) | Not needed |
| **Redcurrants and whitecurrants** | Winter and summer | Not needed |
| **Rhubarb** | No pruning required | Not needed |
| **Strawberries** | Shear off plants after harvesting | Not needed |

# A–Z of fruit

In the following chapter you'll find descriptions of a wide range of fruit and recommended varieties as well as instructions on how to plant and grow them. There is information on feeding, which is essential for all fruit plants, and supporting, which is required by many. The specific pruning requirements for each fruit are also covered here and supplement the general information given in the Pruning chapter (*see* pages 54–73).

# Making choices

There are many fruits that deserve a place in almost any garden. These include apples, strawberries, raspberries, rhubarb, gooseberries and currants. They are relatively easy to grow well and produce good crops of tasty fruit that beat those in the supermarket hands down. Then there are those that should be included, but take a little more effort on the part of the gardener to achieve good crops – for example, pears, blueberries, melons and apricots. The effort might be in the daily care, the pruning or even the harvest. Some will do better with a little protection and others really need a greenhouse or polytunnel for at least some of the year, but on the whole you should be able to grow varieties of all the fruit featured here in normal or sheltered garden conditions.

## What's in a name?

Nowadays there is a huge selection of fruit available from many different suppliers and it can be difficult to make a choice. If you can't find the varieties mentioned in the A–Z, consider what is available, but do some research beforehand – read the catalogue description or get on the internet and check it out. Don't assume the plant will be suitable for your needs: many will be fine, but some might, for example, produce good crops on a tree that is too big for the average garden, while others might bear a reasonable crop only if they are sprayed with chemicals to ward off disease.

## Apples

### harvest JUL, AUG, SEP, OCT

A fruit garden is hardly a fruit garden without an apple, and you can get them in all shapes and sizes, so even the smallest garden can accommodate one (*see* page 15). They are attractive trees with lovely blossom and versatile fruit that often stores well too. You can get eaters (dessert), cookers and dual-purpose varieties, so called because they are good for eating and cooking. The only drawback with apples is that for pollination you may have to grow more than one variety (*see* Pollinating partners box, page 19). 'Family' trees have stems of several varieties grafted onto one rootstock, usually so they produce both cooking and eating apples. This is an option in a very small space but the different varieties often vary in vigour so you can get one taking over.

### Cultivation

DIFFICULTY Depends on how they're grown. Freestanding trees are easiest; supported trees need annual pruning; container-grown trees need regular watering.
PLANT In a sheltered site with fertile, deep, well-drained soil.
SPACE Freestanding trees 3–4.5m (10–15ft) or more apart, depending on the rootstock. Cordons 45cm (18in) apart. Espaliers and stepovers 2m (6ft) or more apart.

CARE Water in after planting. Mulch every spring while the soil is moist. Feed in mid- to late April – sprinkle general-purpose fertilizer in a circle around the base of each tree. Cover an area 90–120cm (3–4ft) in diameter with the trunk as the centre.
STORAGE Store apples in a dryish place that has a constant cool temperature, such as an airy shed or garage. Place them in single layers in shallow, stackable trays that air can circulate around, or put them in large, loose plastic bags with air holes punched in them. Clean, dry fruit in perfect condition should keep until Christmas, but check them regularly and remove any that are starting to go bad before the rot spreads. Alternatively, cook and freeze any surplus.

### Keep them happy by…

Watering dwarf rootstock trees thoroughly in dry spells when they are carrying fruit. Well-established trees on semi-dwarfing rootstocks should not need watering, except in periods of prolonged drought.

Most trees on dwarfing rootstocks must be supported by a stake throughout their life. They also need a circle of weed-free, bare soil around them – 90cm (3ft) in diameter. With more vigorous trees, keep a 90cm (3ft) circle of bare soil around each tree for three to four years to encourage establishment. After that, the grass can be allowed to grow up to the trunk; it will take nitrogen from the soil that might otherwise encourage too much leaf and shoot growth at the expense of fruit production in the trees.

## Pruning

Once the structure is established, freestanding apple trees need very little pruning and your routine will also vary according to the conditions of the previous growing season and the growth that was made – wet seasons tend to mean more pruning. To maintain the health and shape of the tree, remove dead, damaged or diseased wood any time you see it and make an annual check in winter (late October to mid-March). That is also when you should remove overcrowded or badly positioned branches, if necessary. Cut these back to their junction with the trunk or a larger branch. Don't adopt a 'short back and sides' approach, since this encourages masses of strong, leafy, but useless shoots rather than the twiggy growth that carries fruit buds. Thin, spindly growths, known as water shoots, occasionally arise from the trunk; snip these off at their point of origin. Supported trees need annual pruning (see pages 64–8).

Apples have two types of fruiting habit – spur-bearing and tip-bearing. The two types are pruned slightly differently (see opposite and page 78).

## Enjoy them…

As soon as they start ripening – early varieties are ready from late July to September. These early varieties don't keep, so use them straight from the tree. Lift the fruit in your hand and gently twist; if it parts easily from the tree, it's ripe. Leave later varieties on the tree until mid-October, unless high winds are forecast. After picking, store them until you want to use them.

## Look out for…

Maggots in ripe apples are normally codling moth larvae. These tunnel through the developing core and are easy to cut out when preparing fruit for cooking or eating. Hang up codling moth traps from mid-May to mid-August – these are non-chemical pheromone traps that lure the males to a sticky pad, which prevents the females being fertilized – so no maggots. Allow one trap per five trees. The results are not 100 per cent effective, but pheromone traps work better if several neighbours with apple trees all use them.

Scab produces brown or green spots on the foliage, blistered shoots and scabby, distorted fruit. Spray as directed with a suitable fungicide, rake up fallen leaves and prune out badly affected shoots – burn both. Some apple varieties are resistant.

Canker (or Nectria canker) cracks the bark, which shrinks back in flakes, usually in concentric rings. Badly affected branches may die off. Some apple varieties are resistant. Prune out badly affected shoots or even whole branches. Copper-based fungicide helps control it – spray twice in autumn. Bacterial canker is similar (see page 52).

'Bramley's Seedling' is the best-known and most widely grown of all cooking apples. It produces juicy fruit with flesh that melts when cooked.

When they are perfectly ripe, the smell of 'Discovery' apples almost beats their flavour. This is a great eater, but not a very good keeper.

'Greensleeves' is similar to a 'Golden Delicious' apple at its best, with a sharp flavour and crunchy flesh. Its taste deteriorates with keeping.

## HOW TO prune spur-bearing fruit

There are two types of tree: spur-bearing and tip-bearing. Most apples are spur-bearing and carry their fruit in clusters on short branches (spurs) that are at least two years old. Tip-bearing trees are so called because they carry most of their fruit on the tips of shoots produced in the previous season. They need to be pruned differently (*see* page 78).

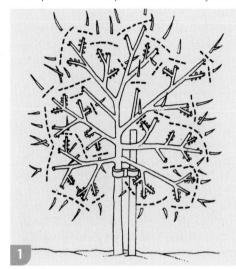

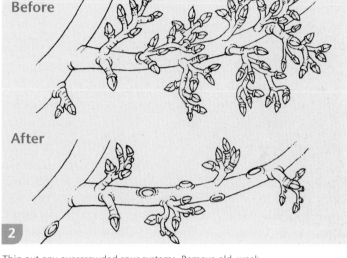

**Before**

**After**

**1** In winter, while the tree is dormant, cut back the end third of each lateral. Prune back new sublaterals on the rest of the framework to five buds, to encourage more fruiting spurs to form.

**2** Thin out any overcrowded spur systems. Remove old, weak spurs and any that develop on the underside of the main branches. Aim for one spur cluster every 10–12cm (4–5in) along the branches.

The rich red-coloured 'Idared' apple has white flesh and can be used as a cooker or an eater. This variety is renowned for its keeping qualities.

Often huge, the fruits of 'James Grieve' are relatively soft-textured with a good flavour. It crops reliably, even in a less than perfect site.

'Winston' is a tough, undemanding tree, producing red apples with firm whitish flesh. The flavour is sharp at first but sweetens as the fruit ages.

Tip-bearing trees are pruned using a renewal method that involves removing some old branches each year, eventually replacing the whole top-growth. Prune in winter, removing a quarter of the oldest fruit-bearing branches and thinning out the centre. Prune the tips of the remaining branches and remove water shoots (fast-growing, straight stems).

Fireblight (see page 52) is a bacterial disease that blackens flowers, leaves and shoots, which wilt as if they had been burned. Oozing cankers may be found on infected stems at blossom time. There is no cure; remove affected branches, taking a good margin of healthy growth too – 30cm (12in) in small branches, 60cm (2ft) in larger ones. Destroy the prunings. Make sure you disinfect your pruning tools. This disease also affects pears, quinces and other members of the rose family, such as cotoneaster and flowering quince (Chaenomeles).

Bitter pit occurs in stored apples (they develop small brown surface spots that may spread through the whole fruit) and is thought to be caused by calcium deficiency and water shortage during growth. Mulch the trees and water well in summer.

## Don't forget

Most apples need a pollinating partner in order to produce fruit (see page 19). A guide to finding pollinating partners is flowering time. Apples that flower around the same time will pollinate each other.

## Worth trying...

**'Ashmead's Kernel'** – Russeted green eating apple with a distinctive pear-drop flavour. Mid- to late-season flowers; harvest from late October but they are traditionally stored to eat from December.

**'Braeburn'** – Crunchy, tangy, red and yellow fruit. Self-fertile; harvest mid-October until just after Christmas.

**'Bramley's Seedling'** – The most popular cooking apple, with large green fruit; crops well in alternate years. Vigorous and easily outgrows small gardens. Mid-season flowers; needs two pollinating partners, but pollination rarely seems a problem. Ready from August, picked fruit keeps well from November to March.

**'Discovery'** – Bright red, small to medium-sized eating apple with crisp flesh when fresh. Early flowers; harvest from late August to late September.

**'Egremont Russet'** – Rough-skinned, pink-flushed, light brown eating apple. Distinctively flavoured, crisp flesh. Early flowers; harvest in October. Will keep but best eaten immediately.

**'Fiesta'** – A crunchy, red eating apple with a zingy flavour. Mid-season flowers; harvest October to November.

**'Greensleeves'** – Medium-sized, green-yellow eating apple, crisp with a sharp flavour. Mid-season flowers; harvest September to November.

**'Howgate Wonder'** – Cooking apple that can also be eaten raw; the flavour appeals to some people but others find it bland. Mid- to late-season flowers; harvest October.

**'James Grieve'** – Cooker and eater with sherbet-flavoured, medium to large, pale yellow fruit streaked with red. Self-fertile. Pick green for cooking from mid-August; leave to ripen for eating from September.

**'Idared'** – Cooker and eater with red fruit that keeps well. Early flowers; harvest from late October.

**'Sunset'** – Eating apple that can replace 'Cox's Orange Pippin' (which is prone to disease and poor cropping) in most situations. Mid-season flowers; harvest late September.

**'Tydeman's Early Worcester'** – Medium-sized, dark red eating and cooking apple with a rich, strawberry-like flavour. Partly self-fertile; early to mid-season flowers; harvest from August.

**'Winston'** – Eating apple with firm, juicy flesh, reminiscent of its 'Cox's Orange Pippin' parent. Disease-resistant. Partly self-fertile with late flowers; harvest October onwards.

**'Worcester Pearmain'** – Aromatic, bright red eating apple with flavoursome, slightly lopsided fruit. Mid-season flowers; harvest from September.

# Apricots

## harvest JUL, AUG, SEP

When they're picked fully ripe from the tree, home-grown apricots are rich, juicy and honey flavoured, with none of the thick, dryish texture of bought versions. They crop well, even in average conditions, and are easier to grow and healthier than their relatives, peaches and nectarines. They will ripen on freestanding trees, but in cold areas grow them as a fan-trained tree against a wall (*see* pages 13–14). Apricots are self-pollinating, so you need grow only one if you're short of space; for very tiny plots, grow a 'patio apricot' in a pot.

## Cultivation

**DIFFICULTY** Easy, given the right conditions; low input.
**PLANT** Choose a sunny, sheltered site with fertile, well-drained soil. Stake securely, using a stake the full height of the trunk.
**SPACE** Those on semi-dwarfing rootstocks (*see* page 15) 4m (13ft) apart. Plant patio varieties in a border 1.2m (4ft) apart.
**CARE** Water regularly until trees are established; mulch generously each spring and apply a general-purpose feed in late April.
**STORAGE** They're best eaten instantly when fully ripe, but can be preserved or frozen in pies.

## Keep them happy by...

Watering trees very well during dry summers. Give them a thorough soaking once a week. Apricot flowers open very early in spring, so protect them if the weather is cold (*see* pages 46–7) and consider hand-pollinating them (*see* page 37).

Thinning a very heavy crop of fruit – remove any deformed or damaged specimens, then take off every third or fourth fruit all over the tree, leaving the remainder well spaced.

## Pruning

Avoid pruning. If you need to remove dead or damaged stems, or shorten long branches, do so in spring or summer, to minimize the risk of silver leaf disease (*see* page 53).

## Enjoy them...

As soon as they are fully ripe; this is when the fruit stops growing and develops a rich, warm flush. Ripe fruit lifts off easily. The fruit on any one tree will ripen over a period of several weeks, so check individual fruits before picking.

## Look out for...

Bacterial canker (*see* page 52) and silver leaf disease (*see* page 53) may affect apricots.

Stem-tips or larger shoots may die back. Prune out affected parts, ideally in spring when growth starts, so it's easy to see exactly how much of a shoot is dead. Cut back to just above a healthy new shoot. 'Moorpark' is often affected.

Patches of a gum-like substance on the surface of healthy bark is called gumming or gummosis and can occur if the tree is stressed, for example in dry conditions or after freezing weather. Mulch and water well in summer; protect the plants adequately in winter (*see* pages 46–7).

## Worth trying...

**'Flavorcot'** – Plum-sized, orange fruit with a reddish flush when ripe in August. Ideal for cooler regions, as it flowers late. On Torinel rootstock (*see* page 15) it makes a heavy-cropping tree about 2–2.5m (6–8ft) tall and 3m (10ft) across.
**'Moorpark'** – Large, pale yellow fruit with a mahogany flush and a scattering of freckles; ready end of August. Often grown on St Julien A (*see* page 15), making a tree 3m (10ft) high and 4.5m (15ft) across.
**'Tomcot'** – Heavy crops of plum-shaped, orange fruit with a red flush in mid-July. Usually grown on Torinel rootstock.

Apricots taste best picked when fully ripe and eaten immediately from the tree. Virtually the only way you can do this is to grow your own.

# Blackberries

**harvest** JUL, AUG, SEP

Although it's hard to beat the joy of rambling along a country hedge picking nature's own provisions on a warm, dry day in late summer, blackberrying in the privacy of your own garden can be very satisfying and you can do it any time you like. The cultivated varieties, which are easy to grow, produce abundant, big, soft and sweetly juicy, mouth-blackening fruit, quite different from the small, often tart wild types. If you lack space there are compact varieties and thornless ones, as well as tempting blackberry hybrids, such as loganberries and tayberries.

Apart from its copious attractive fruit with great flavour, blackberry 'Loch Ness' has no thorns to get snagged on, making it perfect for a small garden.

## Cultivation

**DIFFICULTY** Very easy; little work needed apart from pruning, which takes a few hours each year.

**PLANT** One plant is usually enough (yield is about 4.5kg/10lb from a good modern variety, or 3.6kg/8lb from a very compact form). Blackberries are not too fussy and do well even in exposed areas, on shady walls and on heavy clay soils. Hybrid berries need more shelter and better soil.

**SPACE** Allow a 2m (6ft) run of fence for the most compact varieties, 2.5–4m (8–13ft) for larger modern varieties.

**CARE** Water well until established. Keep the ground well weeded; mulch heavily every spring with well-rotted organic matter, and in late April feed with a general-purpose fertilizer. Use netting to protect ripening fruit from birds.

**STORAGE** Blackberries are best eaten fresh but they freeze well, especially if already cooked, such as in blackberry and apple pie. Alternatively, they make a good jelly or jam.

## Keep them happy by...

Providing very good support. A fence or shed will do fine, but put up some wires to tie them into. Or, erect a post-and-wire support with posts 1.2–1.5m (4–5ft) high (*see* pages 30–1). Allow plenty of space alongside for weeding, picking and pruning. Thornless varieties can be trained over an arch.

## Pruning

**NEW PLANTS** In the first spring, or immediately after planting new canes, prune the strongest, thickest stems to within 25–30cm (10–12in) of soil level. Remove any thin, weak shoots. This will encourage the development of strong, vigorous shoots from the base. As the shoots grow, train them along wires. If any exceed 2m (6ft) long, remove the end 15cm (6in): this will encourage the formation of lateral shoots, which will bear fruit.

**ESTABLISHED PLANTS** Pruning removes old stems that have already borne fruit, makes room for new fruiting canes, and encourages the development of strong, vigorous shoots to replace those that will be removed after fruiting. The annual prune takes place at the same time as training in a new set of canes (*see* opposite) and should be done very shortly after the fruit has been picked.

The training described here creates an open fan with fruiting stems to the left and right and a central bundle of new shoots, which will go to form the fruiting stems next year. This way you can see at a glance which shoots need to be removed after fruiting and which ones should be retained for next year's crop.

## HOW TO prune and train blackberries and their relatives

This is the fan method of training blackberries. (For clarity, leaves are not shown.)

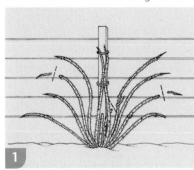

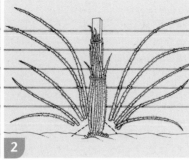

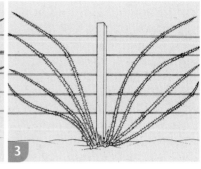

**1** After planting, select the healthiest shoots to train along wire supports about 30cm (12in) apart. Remove damaged or diseased shoot-tips. As new canes grow from the base, tie them loosely to the central post, making a bundle.

**2** Soon after harvest, cut out all the old canes of the fan close to ground level. If left, they will usually become too rampant and won't fruit well, so it is better to replace them with the new stems from the central bundle each year.

**3** Select the strongest canes from the central bundle and train them into a new, well-spaced fan. Remove weak or diseased canes. Leave a central 'parting' for the next generation. In spring, tidy the canes, removing damaged shoot-tips.

### Enjoy them…

As soon as they are ripe – glossy, jet black and slightly soft to the touch, which could be from late summer, depending on which variety you grow. The fruit on any one plant ripens irregularly over several weeks. Allow it to ripen fully on the canes. Loganberries and tayberries tend to ripen earlier than most blackberry varieties; like giant raspberries but with a tarter taste, their fruit turns a deep shade of purplish crimson when it is ripe and ready for picking.

### Look out for…

Raspberry beetles can spoil the fruit of blackberries and loganberries; otherwise, blackberries and their relatives are generally trouble free. Just make sure you pick the fruit regularly before it spoils.

### Worth trying…

#### BLACKBERRIES

'Fantasia' – Huge berries on vigorous, spiny canes; harvest from late August.

'Loch Ness' – Very compact with short, thornless canes that are almost self-supporting. Train like summer-fruiting raspberries (see page 110). Conical berries from mid-August.

'Oregon Thornless' – Decorative leaves and spineless with comparatively well-behaved canes; harvest from late August.

'Veronique' – Very ornamental variety with pink flowers, no thorns, and a compact, semi-upright habit – tie it up to a post or fan it out over a fence panel. Produces good crops of large fruit in late summer.

#### HYBRID BERRIES

Some of these have named varieties with particular qualities, otherwise they are sold under their hybrid name.

'Black Butte' – Long, almost mulberry-like fruit on a fairly compact plant with stems to 2.5m (8ft); harvest from late July.

Boysenberry (blackberry hybrid) – Heavy crops of large, blackberry-like fruit with a wonderful flavour in July and August. More drought-tolerant than true blackberries. Thornless varieties are widely available.

Loganberry (raspberry x dewberry) – Large, red, tangy fruit that is best cooked. The stems may reach 3m (10ft). LY654 is thornless, with large berries from mid-July to early September. LY59 has a good flavour but very thorny stems.

Tayberry (blackberry x raspberry) – Large, rich red fruit, good raw or cooked. Generally considered to be the very best of all the hybrid berries. May reach 3m (10ft). 'Buckingham' is thornless with large, good-quality fruit in July and August.

Tummelberry (tayberry hybrid) – The tayberry-like fruit ripens in mid-July to late August. Much hardier than the tayberry and ideal for more exposed situations.

# Blackcurrants

### harvest JUL, AUG

Tiny packages of vitamin C and bright purple-black juice, blackcurrants are sadly underrated compared to the similar-looking but more glamorous and versatile blueberries. They make a wonderful jam and are great in crumbles and pies, as well as being an excellent component in a mixed fruit juice drink. Try to include at least one bush in your fruit garden; even if you don't make jam you could always use the fruit for concocting interesting sauces. Alternatively, try a jostaberry, which is a cross between a blackcurrant and a gooseberry, with sweet, large fruit.

## Cultivation

**DIFFICULTY** Easy; little work.
**PLANT** In a sunny spot with rich, fertile soil that stays moist – blackcurrants enjoy boggy spots where most fruit won't grow.
**SPACE** 1.5m (5ft) apart; most will reach about 1.2–1.5m (4–5ft) tall.
**CARE** Water well until established. Feed and mulch in spring. Protect ripening fruit from birds using netting in summer.
**STORAGE** They'll keep for a few days in the fridge, otherwise freeze, preserve or make jam.

## Keep them happy by…

Giving them lots of TLC. Blackcurrants are greedy and need a rich diet with lots of moisture, feed and manure. Mulch generously every spring, ideally using well-rotted manure, and feed with a general-purpose fertilizer. In early summer, boost them with a nitrogen-rich feed such as poultry manure pellets, sprinkling two or three handfuls per plant.

## Pruning

The first spring after planting, prune all stems down to a healthy bud (*see* opposite). Thereafter, prune annually in winter, removing one third of the bush. Aiming to remove growth evenly from all around the plant, cut off the oldest stems (the thickest with the darkest bark) and any that are overcrowded or damaged; cut as close to the bottom of the bush as possible.

## Enjoy them…

When they are very ripe and sweet. Leave them on the plants for as long as possible. Pick the whole truss (or 'strig') when all

Blackcurrant 'Ben Sarek' bears heavy crops on a small bush. The berries are comparatively large, which makes picking them less of a chore than with normal-size currants.

the fruit has swelled to maximum size and turned glossy black. Separate individual berries from the thin, wiry stems – one way to do this is to hold the thick end of the stalk and pull the strig through the teeth of a dinner fork, stripping off the berries.

## Look out for…

The small maggots of the gall midge feed on the young leaves, which discolour and are distorted with galls. Pick off and destroy affected leaves.

Big bud mites live inside the buds, making the buds fat and rounded instead of long and slim – this is most obvious in spring, just as new growth starts. The same mites spread reversion disease, which causes unnatural foliage and reduces fruit crops. Check plants each spring and cut off and destroy stems with affected buds. Avoid the problem by growing resistant varieties.

Blister aphids can cause yellow blistering on the leaves (*see* Redcurrants, page 112).

## Worth trying…

'**Ben Connan**' – Very compact yet with large fruit. Some pest and disease resistance.

'**Ben Hope**' – Large crops of medium-sized fruit in July. Pest- and disease-resistant, withstanding gall mites (*see* opposite), so ideal for organic growers. Ripens July.

'**Ben Lomond**' – A heavy cropper producing large fruit at the end of July. Compact and rather upright, it needs very little pruning. '**Ben Nevis**' is similar but the bushes are bigger.

'**Ben Sarek**' – Plentiful crops of large berries from mid-July on dwarf bushes, to 90cm (3ft) high. Fairly frost-resistant flowers.

**Jostaberry** (blackcurrant x gooseberry) – This has all the benefits of both plants with no gooseberry prickles but bigger,

The neat and tidy 'Ben Connan' is a compact plant but it still manages to produce a good crop of delicious-tasting blackcurrants.

sweeter fruit than a blackcurrant. The bush is fairly compact and has resistance to blackcurrant pests and diseases. Best grown on a short trunk or 'leg' 15cm (6in) high and pruned by thinning out a third of the branches each winter.

## HOW TO prune blackcurrants and jostaberries

This is the pruning regime for freestanding plants that produce fruit on the previous year's stems. (For clarity, leaves are not shown.)

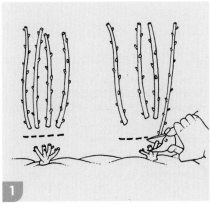

**1**

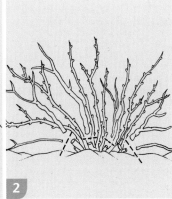

**2**

During the first spring (just as the buds start to swell), or soon after planting, cut down all stems to one healthy bud just above soil level. This will speed establishment. The following winter, cut out any damaged branches, and prune back any thin, weak or small shoots to just above ground level. Thin out any strong shoots that are growing too close together.

In the following and subsequent winters, cut out the oldest fruit-bearing stems as close to ground level as possible, or to just above a strong new shoot low down. Remove any short, thin, weak, damaged or diseased shoots. Renewal pruning may also be carried out after harvest if you prefer.

Jostaberries have gooseberry-sized fruit that is sweeter-tasting than a blackcurrant. As the plants are disease-resistant too, this fruit is well worth a try, especially if you're not growing blackcurrants.

# Blueberries

**harvest** JUL, AUG, SEP

As well as tasting wonderful, blueberries make pretty garden plants with clusters of white bells in late spring, followed by blue fruit then orange-red autumn colour. They do require very acid conditions, so if you have alkaline soil, grow them in large pots of ericaceous compost (*see* page 32). You need two varieties flowering at the same time for effective pollination (*see* page 19).

## Cultivation

**DIFFICULTY** Moderate – you need the right conditions, otherwise little work.

**PLANT** In sun or light dappled shade in rich, fertile, acid soil, ideally in spring.

**SPACE** 1.5m (5ft) apart.

**CARE** Water new plants regularly with soft water or rainwater, and keep them well watered in dry summers. No supports are needed. Each spring give a high-nitrogen feed, and mulch very heavily with well-rotted organic matter; acidic types such as pine needles or bark chippings are best. If plants are slow to make new growth, feed with 25g (1oz) of sulphate of ammonia per plant in late spring or early summer, and water in well.

**STORAGE** They will keep for up to two weeks in shallow layers in the salad drawer of the fridge.

## Keep them happy by…

Adding plenty of organic matter to the soil. The ground needs to be moist but to drain well, so work in grit as well. Use mycorrhizal fungi (sold in sachets and tubs for tree and rose planting) to improve your chances of success. The fungi work with the plant roots for mutual benefit. Add the recommended dose to the bottom of the planting hole and sit the rootball on top so it is in direct contact with the powder.

## Pruning

After planting or in winter, remove any dead or damaged shoots and cut back weak shoots by half to a healthy bud. Do this again the following winter. If you're strong-willed, remove flowers in the first two years to encourage the plant to grow more strongly. Thereafter, prune out one fifth to a quarter of the main stems to the base each year to encourage new wood. Select weak, horizontal or crossing growth.

## Enjoy them…

In midsummer; pick individual fruits as soon as they turn to a deep, bloomy blue-black and feel slightly soft. Depending on the variety you grow, expect to be harvesting from midsummer to early autumn. Plant several varieties for a longer supply.

## Look out for…

Blueberries have no real pest or disease problems in Britain, but they do need careful tending (*see* left).

## Worth trying…

**'Bluecrop'** – Large fruit on bushes 1.2m (4ft) high and 75cm (30in) across. Good for containers.

**'Chandler'** – Very large fruit on bushes 1.5m (5ft) tall.

**'Earliblue'** – Early fruit on bushes up to 2m (6ft) high and 90cm (3ft) wide.

**'Spartan'** – Large, pale blue fruit on bushes up to 2m (6ft) high.

**'Sunshine Blue'** – Heavy crops of flavoursome fruit on 90cm (3ft) plants. Good for containers.

**'Top Hat'** – Smallish fruit but with an excellent flavour on compact bushes 60cm (2ft) high. Good for containers.

Blueberries are very nutritious and they look attractive too. The variety shown here is 'Bluecrop', which is a good choice for containers. Try to grow at least three blueberry plants so that you get a decent supply.

# Cherries

## harvest JUL, AUG, SEP

Until relatively recently, sour cherries, which are suitable for cooking, were the only sensible option for home-growing. Today, thanks to the advent of dwarfing rootstocks (*see* page 15), sweet cherries can also be grown in the average garden. Now the main problem is how to keep the birds away from your fruit – and they're so delicious you won't want to share them. The most straightforward answer is to train the plants in a fan shape (*see* page 21), which can be protected with a net.

## Cultivation

**DIFFICULTY** Easy; low input: crop protection is the main task.
**PLANT** In a sunny, sheltered site with moist but well-drained soil; against a south- or south-west facing wall for fan-training.
**SPACE** Those on ultra-dwarf rootstocks need spacing 2–2.5m (6–8ft) apart, semi-dwarfs 3.5–4.5m (12–15ft) apart and cordons 75cm (30in) apart.
**CARE** Water trees well until they are established, and during dry weather. Each spring, mulch with well-rotted organic matter and in late April sprinkle general-purpose fertilizer over the soil underneath the tree.
**STORAGE** They'll keep for a few days in a salad drawer of the fridge but this spoils the flavour. Make pies and preserves if you need to keep them.

## Keep them happy by...

Planting them in good, deep, fertile soil; they really do not thrive in sandy or shallow soils. Avoid cold or exposed sites too.

## Pruning

Avoid pruning cherries if possible, as this encourages silver leaf disease (*see* page 53). Select well-shaped, freestanding trees or ready-trained fans or cordons.

## Enjoy them...

When they are fully ripe (allow them to develop their full colour on the tree). Snip the stems with scissors or secateurs.

## Look out for...

Blackfly congregate round the tips of young shoots, particularly in late spring. Wipe them off with damp kitchen roll where possible, or use an organic pesticide.

'Stella' is the perfect cherry for the home gardener – it is self-fertile, with cherry-red to almost black fruit that has a sweet, juicy flavour.

Bacterial canker (*see* page 52) can be very serious in cherries and may kill young specimens.

Silver leaf (*see* page 53) is a major problem of plants in the genus *Prunus* and can also affect cherries.

## Worth trying...

**'Morello'** – The most popular sour cherry. Self-fertile, with huge crops of large, red fruit, excellent for cooking, in August or September. It crops well, even when grown against a north-facing wall, as long as there is reasonable light.
**'Stella'** – Self-fertile, sweet cherry with dark red fruit that ripens from mid-July to August.
**'Sunburst'** – Sweet, self-fertile variety with large, black cherries in early July.
**'Sweetheart'** – Modern, self-fertile, sweet cherry with dark red fruit, which is ready for harvesting in late August, long after most other sweet varieties have finished fruiting. Ideal for home gardeners, since the fruit ripens over several weeks, which staggers your harvest.

# Citrus fruit

harvest **JUL, AUG, SEP, OCT**

Fresh lemons have a far more intense flavour and much softer skins than those you buy in the shops. They're fun to grow, but you'll never be overwhelmed with fruit. However, lemons and other citrus fruit make superb plants in large pots or tubs on a patio in summer. They are evergreen, with scented flowers that start opening early in spring and continue on and off all summer. Citrus plants are spiny, so make sure they're out of the way of thoroughfares, and bring them indoors in winter.

## Cultivation

**DIFFICULTY** Easy; moderate input.
**PLANT** They must stay in a pot and, unlike many other plants, prefer to be slightly pot bound.
**CARE** Correct watering is crucial (*see* below). Feed regularly from April to August using special citrus feed or a high-nitrogen liquid feed. Feed monthly for the rest of the year with a general-purpose liquid feed.

Repot young plants in April, but only if the old pot is really packed full of roots. Use a special citrus compost (available from garden centres) or use John Innes No. 2 potting compost mixed with lime-free potting grit or perlite (in a ratio of 3:1). Only move them up one pot size at a time. Top-dress older plants in large containers every year or two in spring: scrape away the top few centimetres of compost and replace it with new citrus compost or a home-made equivalent.
**STORAGE** You probably won't get enough fruit to need to worry about storage, but fresh ripe lemons will keep in a fruit bowl for several weeks.

## Keep them happy by...

Watering properly. Always give the plants a thorough soaking when their compost is almost dry, then wait until it reaches the same stage before watering again. Preferably use rainwater and avoid tap water if possible. If you must use it, run the water through a jug-type filter or boil and cool it.

All citrus plants dislike dramatic changes, so make any changes to their growing conditions gradual. In winter, lemons need a minimum temperature of 7°C (45°F) and good light; other citrus plants need 10°C (50°F). They like some humidity but also good ventilation. They are better outside between June and late September, where they are less prone to pests.

Even without the wonderful fruit, it's worth growing a lemon for the intoxicating fragrance of its flowers. 'Meyer's Lemon', which is thought to have a mandarin orange in its parentage, flowers more or less all year round.

Acclimatize them carefully, putting them in a lightly shady spot to begin with. Eventually stand them in a warm, sheltered spot that gets some sun, though not the strongest midday sun.

If grown in a conservatory all year round, try to keep the temperature below 29°C (85°F) in summer.

## Pruning

Initial pruning aims to get a bushy plant with balanced growth and a well-developed framework of branches, but you'll often find that you buy your plant like this anyway. After this, no major pruning is required. The stems may be bare after winter leaf fall, so branches and shoots can be shortened by up to two thirds every other year. The best time to prune a citrus plant is in early spring, but if the plant has flowers and fruit on the shoots at this time, it's better to trim back little and often throughout the year.

## Enjoy them...

When fruits are ripe. Wait for them to reach full size then watch for their colour to deepen. This can take two or more months. Squeeze regularly to check for ripeness and don't allow them to go soft. You can pick most citrus fruits slightly unripe as they will continue to ripen off the tree. Use secateurs to remove them, complete with stalk.

Though sour to eat, the fruit of the Calamondin orange can be used to make juice, and it's popular in south-east Asian cooking.

The lime variety 'Tahiti' is known as the bartender's lime but is also excellent for using in cooking. It has no pips and a zingy but sweet flavour.

The neat little fruits of the kumquat have a sweet and sour taste. Crunch them whole, add them to fruit salad or you could use them for garnish.

## Look out for...

Cultivation problems, such as few flowers, sparse fruit and yellowing leaves, are the most common cause of things going wrong with citrus fruit; you may be keeping the plant too wet, repotting before it's necessary or into a container that's too large, or constantly changing the growing conditions.

Scale insects make the foliage sticky, often with black, powdery patches. They are tiny, buff-coloured 'limpets' on the stems and undersides of leaves. Remove by hand using cotton buds, or use a spray (preferably organic). They are far less of a problem on plants that live outside in summer. The black deposit on the leaves is sooty mould, which grows on the sticky honeydew secreted by the insects. It sponges off.

## Worth trying...

### LEMONS

'Lemonade' – A compact lemon with good crops of medium-sized, delicately flavoured fruit.

'Meyer's Lemon' – Easy, reliable and cold-tolerant, this lemon variety is more compact than most and can flower all year round. Widely available.

'Variegated' – More delicate than most, this lemon has beautiful green and cream leaves and fruit with green and yellow stripes. It needs warmer conditions than many; best kept

at 10°C (50°F) in winter and should be put outside only in an exceptionally warm, sheltered spot, if at all.

### OTHER CITRUS PLANTS

Many of these are available only at specialist nurseries or by mail order.

**Calamondin orange** (x *Citrofortunella microcarpa*) – More often grown for its decorative value, the small fruit of this shrubby tree is sour, but the skin is sweet.

**Citron** (*Citrus medica*) – The large, uneven fruit of this sizeable plant are used for making candied peel. It is also highly aromatic, so worth drying to add to pot-pourri.

**Kaffir lime** (*Citrus hystrix*) – The leaves of this lime are used in Thai cooking.

**Kumquat** (*Fortunella japonica*) – This close relation to the citrus family is a compact, bushy plant with small, bitter-tasting, oval orange fruit.

**Lime** (*Citrus aurantiifolia*) – 'Tahiti' is fairly compact and the most reliable variety, producing scented flowers and small, sweet fruit – good in a gin and tonic!

**Orange** (*Citrus sinensis*) – These are usually large plants with scented flowers and fruit that is slower to grow and ripen than lemons. 'Valencia' is grown for its large, almost seedless fruit, which ripens in time for Christmas.

# Cranberries

harvest **SEP, OCT**

Although not the most versatile of fruits, cranberries do have their place, especially for making sauces and juices, and the low, sprawling plants are attractive, particularly when in flower as they have pretty, bell-shaped pink blooms. In the wild, they live on heaths in very acidic, semi-boggy sites; at home, you'll need to recreate these conditions, most probably in pots. Cranberries require even more acidic conditions than blueberries.

## Cultivation

**DIFFICULTY** Easy; success depends on giving them a sufficiently acidic growing medium (*see* page 32).
**PLANT** In pots of ericaceous compost mixed with about 10 per cent lime-free grit (you can find this in sand and gravel sections in garden centres). Use a 38–45cm (15–18in) pot for each cranberry plant.

While you wouldn't want to eat them raw, cranberries are great stewed for sauces or to make a tangy, vitamin-packed topping to a bowl of vanilla ice cream.

**CARE** Water well and carefully (*see* below). Feed every week or so from April to August using a soluble product especially formulated for acid-loving plants.
**STORAGE** They freeze very well, either untouched as whole fruit or as a sauce.

## Keep them happy by...

Standing the pot in a deep, water-filled saucer to maintain the bog-like conditions of the plant's natural habitat, and watering with rainwater rather than tap water, which is too limy and alkaline.

## Pruning

No pruning is needed. Cut back any long, lanky shoots in spring to tidy if necessary.

## Enjoy them...

As they turn bright red in late September and October. You can leave them on the plant until you need them.

## Look out for...

As long as they get the right growing conditions they will not have any problems.

## Worth trying...

It can be difficult to obtain plants and you may need to use mail order. They are often unnamed but **'Early Black'** has medium-sized, very dark blackish-red fruit and **'Pilgrim'** is similar with paler fruit.

Cranberries make an attractive pot plant with their small, almost heather-like, pale green leaves and pretty bell flowers followed by shiny bright red fruit.

# Figs

**harvest AUG, SEP**

It is possible to produce wonderful figs at home and the plants are very attractive. However, they must be firmly pruned in order to bear plenty of fruit. Figs are deciduous, shrubby plants and grow best in a warm, sunny position, with some protection from severe frost. They can produce three crops of fruit each year, although only one crop is likely to reach maturity.

## Cultivation

**DIFFICULTY** Easy (once established); moderate input.
**PLANT** Outdoors against a south-facing wall with humus-rich, well-drained soil. Restrict the root-run (*see* page 90). In a small garden grow a standard fig in a 38–45cm (15–18in) pot filled with John Innes No. 3 potting compost on a hot patio. Under glass grow figs in pots to keep them compact.
**SPACE** For a fan-trained fig allow at least 2m x 2m (6ft x 6ft) of wall or fence space. A fig grown in the open garden may reach 3m (10ft) high and wide. In pots they can be restricted to 1.2–1.5m (4–5ft) high.

'Brown Turkey' is the classic fig for home growers. It produces soft, plump, tear-shaped fruit with a brown tinge and has an excellent flavour and texture.

**CARE** A fan-trained, root-restricted fig needs a spring feed (use general-purpose fertilizer) and a generous mulch. Water well from spring until autumn. Pot-grown figs need plenty of water, and feed them from spring to autumn using tomato feed or something similar. If they dry out they will drop their crop.

## HOW TO create a fig bush

With young figs it is often necessary to prune initially to produce a clear stem of 1.2m (4ft), with the branches evenly spaced above.

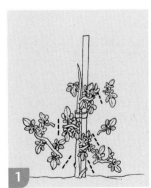
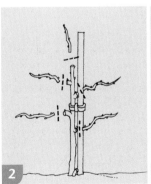

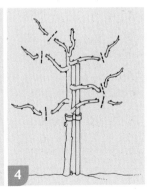

**1** In the first spring, cut down all growth to 10–15cm (4–6in) above compost level. As it grows, train the strongest new shoot up a cane. Remove the lower shoots and in summer prune back growing laterals to four leaves.

**2** In the second spring, prune the laterals to a single bud. Reduce the central leader by one third, cutting to a strong bud. Summer prune as before. The third spring, remove the tip of the leader, and cut back all the laterals to a single bud.

**3** In the fourth spring, as new shoots grow, select five or six of the healthiest and allow these to develop into a branched framework, evenly spaced around the main stem. If a new upright leader starts to form, cut it back to four buds.

**4** In the fifth spring, shorten the framework branches to six buds. Remove any growth that might make a new central leader and, if they are present on the tree, cut out any sucker growths or laterals below the tree's head.

STORAGE The fruit is so delicious eaten straight from the tree that you won't want to store it, but you can preserve individual fruits in syrup.

## Keep them happy by…

Pruning them to maintain shape and size, and restricting the root-run by planting inside a large sunken container, such as three paving slabs formed into a box against the house wall, or a planting hole lined with bricks and rubble. This stops the tree from growing large and leafy instead of fruiting well. Otherwise, grow figs in containers.

Top-dress pot-grown figs each spring, scraping away 2.5cm (1in) of the old compost and replacing it with fresh John Innes No. 3 containing some slow-release fertilizer. They will need repotting into a slightly larger tub every four to five years, but delay it as long as possible since figs fruit best when they are pot bound.

Pot-grown figs can survive outdoors on a sheltered, sunny patio, but do better if brought into a greenhouse or conservatory for the winter.

## Pruning

Prune in spring, thinning growth and limiting the size of the plant (*see* below). For fan-training figs, *see* pages 67–8.

## Enjoy them…

When they have fully ripened on the plant from late August on. Outdoor figs ripen at the rate of a few every day over several weeks. They soften and change colour (turning brown or purple), and the 'eye' on the bottom is open. The ideal moment is just before the fruit falls off the tree naturally. The insides should be moist and sticky. If they're dry and mealy you're a few days too early.

## Look out for…

Figs have few problems, but must be kept well watered otherwise you'll lose the fruit.

## Worth trying…

'Brown Turkey' – Large crops of medium-sized, purplish-tinged, brown figs with red flesh inside. The most widely sold and recommended for growing outdoors.

'Brunswick' – Greeny-gold skins are flushed brown when the fruit is ripe and the flesh is yellow inside. Not as widely available as 'Brown Turkey'.

'White Marseilles' – Large, very deeply lobed leaves and big, pear-shaped, green-tinged, white fruit. Suitable for a very warm, sheltered spot outside but needs bringing under cover for protection in winter.

## HOW TO maintain a fig bush

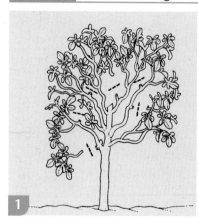

1. In spring, shorten the framework branches to six buds. Remove any growth that might make a new central leader and any sucker growths or laterals below the head of the tree.

2. In summer, shorten all the sublaterals from the main framework of branches back to five leaves, and pinch out any new shoots at five or six leaves to encourage fruit formation.

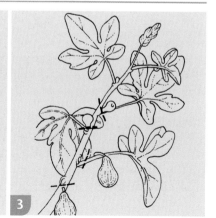

3. In early autumn, remove any fruit larger than small pea size as these won't develop. Leave the remaining fruits to overwinter (cover the plant with fleece if necessary); usually they will ripen the following year.

# Gooseberries

**harvest** MAY, JUN, JUL

Gooseberries are prickly little shrubs with hairy green, yellow or pinkish fruits that are great for making traditional desserts and jams as well as for eating as a fresh fruit. Dessert gooseberries are relative newcomers, but very welcome and completely delicious, cooked or raw. If you are going to grow only one gooseberry, make it a dessert variety. You can grow gooseberries as conventional bushes, as double cordons against a warm, sunny wall, or as standards in borders or pots.

## Cultivation

**DIFFICULTY** Easy; moderate input.
**PLANT** In a sunny, sheltered place in well-drained, fertile soil.
**SPACE** 90cm (3ft) apart if they are to be conventional bushes or standards or 45cm (18in) apart between cordons.
**CARE** Each spring, add a generous mulch underneath the plants and in mid- to late April sprinkle on a general-purpose fertilizer. Water in dry spells in summer.
**STORAGE** Cook them and use in pies or jams. Cooking and dessert varieties can be frozen as they are.

## Keep them happy by…

Thinning the fruit in stages between late May and June. You can cook the removed fruits. Leave half the original crop evenly spaced over the bush to fill out and ripen fully.

## Pruning

Cut all the stems of gooseberry bushes back by half after planting. Do other pruning from November to February, with a little manicuring in summer (*see* page 70).

## Enjoy them…

Pick the green cooking varieties as soon as they are big enough, often as early as May. The smaller the gooseberries, the more sour they taste, so you'll need more sugar when cooking them. Dessert gooseberries are not completely ripe until July.

## Look out for…

American gooseberry mildew forms a white, powdery 'bloom' over the tips of young shoots, leaves and fruit. Wipe this off the fruit and prune out the affected tips of shoots after the fruit has been picked. Prevent mildew by pruning to improve air

'Greenfinch' makes a compact bush with a reliable crop of green cooking gooseberries. Its disease resistance means organic specimens are available.

circulation around the plants, and feed with 28g (1oz) of sulphate of potash per plant in spring instead of general-purpose fertilizer. Grow resistant varieties.

The 'looper' caterpillars of the magpie moth (white, with black and orange markings) can strip the bushes of leaves in May and June. Remove them by hand on sight.

Dull khaki caterpillars, about 2.5cm (1in) long on the leaf undersides from early May into late summer, are the larvae of the gooseberry sawfly. A bad infestation can quickly defoliate the bushes. Again, remove them by hand on sight.

Birds love dessert gooseberries so use netting (*see* pages 46–7).

## Worth trying…

'**Greenfinch**' – Smooth green fruit; compact, mildew-resistant.
'**Hinomaki Red**' – Large, sweet dessert fruit that ripens to red in July. Mildew-resistant. '**Hinomaki Yellow**' ripens to pale gold.
'**Invicta**' – A traditional thorny variety with heavy crops of tasty, tangy green fruit in June. Mildew-resistant.
'**Pax**' – Heavy cropping, thornless, red dessert gooseberry. Mildew-resistant.
'**Whinham's Industry**' – Similar to 'Pax' but thorny; succeeds in shade and heavy soil where others would not.

# Grapes

## Indoors
**harvest** SEP, OCT, NOV

## Outdoors
**harvest** AUG, SEP, OCT

Grapes are attractive plants for both indoors in a conservatory or greenhouse, or outdoors, rambling on a warm wall, cordon-grown over a pergola or properly trained on a system of posts and wires. To be sure of getting a reasonable crop you need to pay great attention to pruning, and be hard-hearted enough to remove flowers and young grapes, but it's perfectly possible to get well-flavoured fruit with a bit of care.

## Cultivation

**DIFFICULTY** Easy to demanding, depending on how you grow them.

**PLANT** In a warm, sunny, sheltered spot, such as against a south-facing fence or wall, in well-drained soil that is fertile and contains plenty of well-rotted organic matter. (*See* box, opposite, for growing grapes indoors.)

**SPACE** 1.5m (5ft) apart in rows 2–2.5m (6–8ft) apart.

**CARE** Mulch generously each spring and sprinkle a handful of general fertilizer, and 15g (½oz) of sulphate of potash over the soil around the base of each vine in April. Keep vines well watered in dry spells during the summer while they are carrying fruit, particularly when growing the plants against a wall or fence, since this shelters them from some natural rainfall; foundations will restrict their root-run.

**STORAGE** They will keep for up to two weeks in the fridge and can be frozen whole and used to make smoothies.

## Keep them happy by…

Attending carefully to pruning, *see* below and pages 71–2.

## Pruning

**INFORMAL TRAINING** When growing a vine informally, allow it to scramble over trellis or secure the main stems to the uprights of a pergola and let the rest run freely over the top. Once the vine has had a year or two to form a woody framework, it will start producing flowers followed by grapes. If it's possible to reach them easily, it's worth limiting them to four bunches per vine, at least for the first year or two, otherwise the fruit will

Black grapes are particularly attractive in the garden when they are in fruit. 'Boskoop Glory' is considered one of the best for growing outdoors in our variable climate.

be small and pippy. In midwinter (December/January), when the vine is dormant and leafless, thin out overcrowded growth to keep it tidy and within its allotted space.

**FORMAL TRAINING** For proper pruning and training there is little to beat the double Guyot or renewal method (*see* pages 17 and 94). It involves pruning and training shoots emerging from a short, original main stem to create two horizontal rods from which fruiting shoots are trained vertically on a system of wires. This is more labour-intensive than the cordon method (*see* pages 71–2), but it's very useful for producing large quantities of good-quality grapes in a small area. (For support information, *see* pages 30–1.)

Repeat the process each year. For the first few seasons, restrict the number of flowers each fruiting shoot produces. As the plant matures, and its 'leg' thickens, it can bear more flower trusses.

## Enjoy them…

Completely ripe, so leave them a little while after they have changed colour. Depending on the variety cultivated, you can be picking grapes as early as late August and as late as the end of October. Cut the whole bunch (test for ripeness first).

If you like green grapes and fancy trying wine-making, 'Müller Thurgau' is a good choice, producing large and attractive bunches that make a crisp dry wine.

## Look out for…

Birds will happily eat all of an outdoor crop, so protect bunches with small nets or whole plants with a sheet of netting.

## Worth trying…

'**Boskoop Glory**' – A reliable black grape for both wine-making and eating.

'**Brandt**' – This is a dual-purpose, ornamental and dessert grape with small bunches of small, sweet, black grapes. Great autumn foliage colour. Good for a pergola or trellis; crops without undue attention.

'**Dornfelder**' – Large, sweet, dark red grapes in good-sized bunches in early autumn.

'**Müller Thurgau**' – The classic home-grown wine vine, but also good for eating in dry summers when planted in a warm, sunny spot or against a sunny wall.

'**Perlette**' – Thin-skinned, sweet and seedless green grapes that ripen early.

'**Strawberry**' – Bunches of copper-pink to amber fruit that ripens late in the season. As its name suggests, the flavour is considered to be similar to that of strawberries.

## Growing grapes indoors

Greenhouse grapevines are traditionally planted with their roots outside in a prepared bed. The main stem is led inside through a hole in the wall. Alternatively, plant a vine in a large tub of John Innes No. 3 potting compost or in a bed of rich soil inside. It will need an area at least 2–2.5m (6–8ft) wide. Water well from March onwards, increasing the quantity especially when the vine is carrying a crop. Each spring sprinkle 25–50g (1–2oz) of general-purpose feed and 15–25g (½–1oz) of sulphate of potash over the soil where the roots are growing. In a pot, scrape off the top few centimetres of soil and replace it with new John Innes No. 3 into which you've mixed a dose of slow-release feed. Use liquid tomato feed once a week during the growing season too. You'll need to pollinate the grapes by hand (*see* page 37).

For how to prune and train grapes, *see* pages 71–2. You can stop the vine at a convenient height. In late January or early February, when vine buds first start developing, cut the ties that hold the rod to the wall and lay it flat on the ground for two weeks before tying it back up. This encourages buds to develop right the way along the rod, so you have fruit-bearing laterals all the way up instead of only near the top of the plant.

With bigger grapes, thin the fruit when they are pea-sized. Use special vine scissors or nail scissors with long, narrow blades, and snip out every other grape, taking care not to damage those that are left. Seedless grapes don't need thinning.

Among the best indoor varieties are 'Schiava Grossa' ('Black Hamburgh'), which produces large bunches of big, sweet black grapes and 'Buckland Sweetwater', which has large amber grapes. 'Muscat of Alexandria' needs heat at the end of the summer to ripen, but has grapes of superior quality and flavour – for the connoisseur. 'Perlette' is good indoors as well as out.

'Schiava Grossa' is a popular indoor variety with large bunches of big, sweet grapes. It is fast-growing and reliable and has wonderful autumn foliage.

## HOW TO train and maintain vines by the double Guyot renewal method

In the first winter after planting the vine, cut the stem down to about 15cm (6in) above ground level or, in the case of a grafted vine, 15cm (6in) above the swollen graft union.

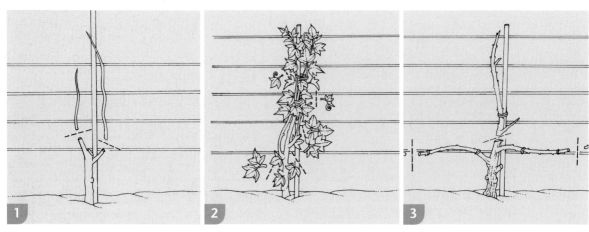

**1** In the first spring, select two strong shoots and tie them to a vertical support. Remove any other shoots that develop. In late autumn or early winter, reduce the two shoots to about 8cm (3in) long, cutting just above a bud. You will be left with a stumpy main stem, or 'leg'.

**2** In the second spring, as new growth begins, select three strong shoots growing from the top of the leg; remove all the others. Tie these shoots loosely to the upright cane. Remove any tendrils that form, and cut back to one leaf any other shoots growing from the selected stems.

**3** After leaf fall, tie the two strongest stems to the bottom wire and reduce them to 60cm (2ft). Prune the remaining third stem to 8cm (3in), above a bud. In the third spring, allow the horizontal stems to produce three fruiting shoots each; rub out any other shoots.

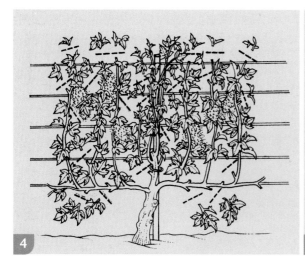

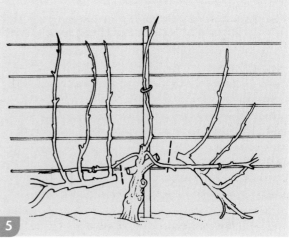

**4** In the third summer, vertically train three shoots from each horizontal stem. Pinch them out when they reach the height of the third wire and remove any sideshoots. Let only one cluster of flowers set fruit on each shoot. Allow three new shoots to grow from the top of the central stem. From the fourth year onwards, let the vertical shoots grow two leaves beyond the top wire and allow up to three flower clusters per shoot.

**5** Every winter, remove the horizontal and vertical stems that fruited in the summer. Bring down the two strongest of the three central stems to replace them. These will produce new fruiting shoots in the coming growing season. Cut back the third stem. This will result in new shoots growing from the top of the central stem, from which you will once again select three strong stems to become the replacement shoots for the following year.

# Kiwi fruit

## harvest OCT

Despite their rather unpromising outward appearance, kiwis are a delicious, juicy, tangy fruit and well worth trying at home, especially now that self-fertile outdoor varieties are available. Before this you had to grow at least two plants indoors – and they may be attractive but they are also big, with a tendency to take over when your back's turned. Outdoors they make a decorative addition to the garden when trained up a sunny pergola, wall or fence. Besides keeping them within reasonable bounds, pruning also encourages them to produce more fruit.

## Cultivation

**DIFFICULTY** Easy; moderate input.
**PLANT** In a warm, sunny, sheltered spot with humus-rich, fertile, well-drained soil.
**SPACE** Allow 3–4.5m (10–15ft) all around each plant.
**CARE** Mulch generously in spring, and sprinkle a handful of general-purpose fertilizer and 15g (½oz) of sulphate of potash over the soil under each plant in April. Pay attention to pruning (*see* below and page 96).
**STORAGE** Arrange the fruit in a single layer in trays in a cool room, garage or shed, where they should keep for up to six weeks. The flavour will also continue to develop.

### Keep them happy by…

Providing a strong framework of trellis or wires to grow on and training them properly. Tie in new growth regularly during summer.

Also, it helps to mulch generously in spring to keep up soil fertility. These are vigorous plants and need plenty of food to keep up their growth rates.

### Pruning and training

Kiwis are best trained as espaliers on horizontal wires about 30–45cm (12–18in) apart (*see* pages 65–6). The aim is to create a number of tiers of horizontal stems that will carry fruiting spurs. The vines need frequent tying in as they grow very rapidly, but this must be done after the new shoot has hardened enough not to break when it is bent into position. Tie the stems to the supports; don't allow them to twine.

Prune in late winter or early spring, after the risk of severe frost has passed (there may be some bleeding, but this does not seem to harm the plant) and again in summer. The idea is to continually replace shoots that are older than three or four years.

If you don't have room for many kiwi fruit plants, have one of each sex and plant both in the same hole. Train them in the same way, but have one upright stem for each plant and train alternate male and female stems out along your wires.

### Enjoy them…

In October, or later if it has been a poor summer. Pick one or two occasionally to try – they should be softly firm and will taste sweet. If an early frost or severe weather is forecast, drape fleece over the plants so the fruit can continue ripening (*see* page 46).

### Look out for…

Problems with cultivation, such as small fruit that doesn't ripen. This is usually due to the plant being cold or receiving too little sun. In an exposed or northerly site, grow kiwis indoors on the sunny side of a greenhouse or conservatory.

### Worth trying…

**'Abbott'** and **'Bruno'** – Both have good crops; fruit of 'Bruno' is slightly larger; both need pollinating partners (*see* page 19).
**'Jenny'** – Self-fertile with small, very sweet fruit. Not very hardy.
**'Hayward'** – Not over-vigorous and flowers quite late; 'Tomuri' is a good pollinating partner.

Kiwis are a comparative newcomer to British fruit gardens but should crop well, as long as they are kept under control with careful pruning. 'Bruno' (left) has large, longish fruit.

## HOW TO train kiwi fruit

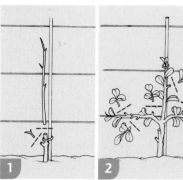

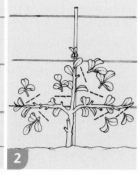

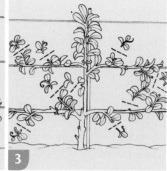

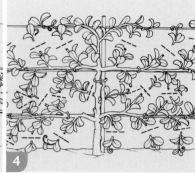

**1** During winter, or soon after planting, cut the main stem back to about 30cm (12in) high and remove any other shoots that are competing with it.

**2** As the new growth starts, select the three strongest shoots. Tie one to the cane to keep as the main stem, and train the other two horizontally along the lowest wires. Remove any other shoots.

**3** In summer, prune the laterals back to 90cm (3ft). Allow sublaterals to develop on them at 50cm (20in) intervals, and cut these back to five leaves to form fruiting spurs. If suitable laterals appear higher up the main stem, train them horizontally on the next wire.

**4** The following summer, after cutting back the main stem to the wire above the topmost laterals, select the strongest shoots from it to form the next tier of laterals. On these, allow fruiting shoots to form and prune them as on the lower laterals. Continue each year until the desired size is reached.

## Siberian kiwi

The Siberian kiwi or Mongolian gooseberry (*Actinidia arguta* 'Issai') is more compact than conventional kiwis and has small, sweet, smooth-skinned, gooseberry-sized fruit that ripens more reliably and slightly earlier. It's ideal for colder or smaller gardens. Grow the plant as a single slanting or horizontal stem tied to a supporting pole or on a wire across a fence or shed, and prune the laterals to 20cm (8in) long each winter to form branching fruiting spurs. Alternatively, more decoratively, train it round an obelisk or topiary frame in a border or a large tub on the patio.

## HOW TO maintain kiwi fruit

**1** In summer, shorten sublaterals to five leaves beyond the fruit. Cut back any bare, unproductive lengths of growth to five leaves, and any new shoots growing around the fruiting spurs to seven leaves.

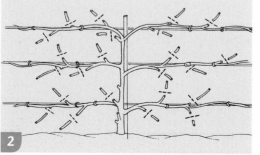

**2** In midwinter, prune fruiting shoots to two or three buds beyond the point where the last fruit was borne. On older vines, cut back three-year-old fruiting shoots to a dormant bud or new shoot at the base.

# Melons

Melons are so tempting to grow and so dependent on a warm summer to do well, but anticipation is half the excitement. Cantaloupe types (*see* page 98), which are small, round and with marked segments or textured skin, are most likely to be successful. They generally need an unheated greenhouse or a cold frame, but in a hot summer you can experiment with letting them run along the ground outdoors.

## Cultivation

**DIFFICULTY** Intermediate to hard; something of a challenge.
**SOW** In small individual pots on a warm windowsill indoors in early or mid-April. When the pots are full of roots, choose the strongest plants and pot them on into 10cm (4in) pots. Each plant needs a cane to grow up. Tie them in gently with soft twine; it is very easy to damage the stems. Keep them on a light windowsill, or move them to a heated propagator (with a tall lid) at 16°C (60°F) in a greenhouse or conservatory. Harden them off slowly for two or three weeks from late April.
**PLANT** In a greenhouse or conservatory in mid- to late May into pots, growbags or dug and enriched greenhouse borders. On a patio, plant against a sunny wall in late May or early June in pots of multipurpose compost. Alternatively, plant in early to mid-June in a warm, well-sheltered, sunny area of your fruit garden in well-drained, very humus-rich ground; cover with a cloche or cold frame.
**SPACE** 45cm (18in) apart for plants to be trained vertically up canes or walls; allow 90cm (3ft) between plants running on the ground.
**CARE** Water young plants very sparingly when they are first planted and increase gradually as growth takes off. Too much water too soon can cause rotting at the base. When the first flower opens, start feeding weekly with a liquid general-purpose feed; change to liquid tomato feed when the first fruit starts swelling. Increase to twice weekly when the plants are carrying two or more fruits.
**STORAGE** Don't store them; instead, eat them sun-warm, fresh from the garden.

## Keep them happy by…

Making sure they never suffer from the cold. Melon plants are very sensitive to cold, which stops them growing for a while,

As it ripens, the skin of a 'Sweetheart' melon becomes very pale and the stripes are more distinct. This is a good choice for trying outdoors in a sheltered, sunny site.

and they will be killed by the slightest hint of frost. Have some fleece handy to cover plants if the weather takes a bad turn.

Give plants good support – trellis or netting is suitable – and tie the stems with soft twine. Plants grown in cold frames or allowed to run over the ground will do best if given some stout, plastic-coated netting supported on bricks or logs to ramble over. This lifts the stems and developing fruit off the ground to avoid rotting. Support plants grown in a greenhouse by training the stems up canes or strings attached to the roof.

Cantaloupe melons can succeed outdoors in Britain if given a warm, dry summer. Here, landscaping fabric suppresses weeds and provides some protection against damaging rots that are encouraged by damp soil.

**Don't forget**

Don't grow melons in the same greenhouse as cucumbers; melons cross-pollinate with cucumbers, which will become extremely bitter and misshapen as a result.

If your melons are growing under cover, ensure pollination by doing it yourself (*see* box, page 37).

Allow sideshoots to grow, since this is where the flowers form, but pinch out their growing-tips two leaves beyond a developing melon to stop plants outgrowing the space, and to encourage the plant to put its energy into swelling up the fruit.

## Enjoy them…
From August to early October, when you can smell a musky scent on their skin that tells you they are ripe. To be sure, hold the fruit in your palms and use the tips of your thumbs gently to press the bottom (furthest from the stalk) – a ripe fruit gives slightly. Use secateurs to snip through the short stem that connects the fruit to the plant.

## Look out for…
Cold, wet conditions or disease may cause neck rot. Suspect this if newly planted melon plants wither and die – pull them

out and you'll see the roots have vanished or have rotted off at the neck of the plant. Plant melons on small soil mounds with a 'moat' at the base and water sparingly, into the moat, until plants are established and growing well.

Avoid growing melons or cucumbers in the same soil several years running and don't grow them in the same greenhouse, since they will cross-pollinate and the flavour of both will suffer.

## Worth trying…
**'Amber Nectar'** (syn. 'Castella') – Net-skinned, striped fruit with wonderful-tasting, sweet orange flesh. Reliable inside or out, capable of producing several reasonable-sized melons.
**'Galia'** – Like the galias you can buy, these have netted, greeny skin and pale green, fragrant flesh. Best in a greenhouse or under a cold frame, because they really need warmth.
**'Sweetheart'** – Smooth, pale green skins and pale orange, delicately flavoured flesh. Reliable in the garden, greenhouse or cold frame.

# Mulberries

## harvest AUG, SEP

Black mulberries deserve a special spot in the garden as they make wonderful spreading trees with rough bark and large, heart-shaped leaves, and produce the most fantastic fruit. If you like eating mulberries you really have to grow your own since they don't travel well. Be warned though – the tree can end up very large.

## Cultivation

**DIFFICULTY** Easy; low input.

**PLANT** In a sheltered site in fertile, well-drained soil. They make a good freestanding specimen or an excellent espalier.

**SPACE** Trees eventually reach about 6m (20ft) all round, but they take their time.

**CARE** Stake a newly planted tree until it is well established (four or five years). An espalier needs permanent support (*see* pages 30–1). Water a new plant regularly during the first summer, especially if it's hot and dry; thereafter, a freestanding tree needs watering only in a dry summer when it is carrying fruit. An espalier will always need regular watering.

**STORAGE** Possible as jam or jellies, or frozen, but they're best eaten fresh and raw.

## Keep them happy by...

Providing a sunny spot and not pruning unless really necessary, as the branches 'bleed' sap when cut. As they get older, mulberries become craggy and gnarled and tend to collapse outwards. They can be seen like this in old gardens, supported on stakes to prevent the branches from breaking. Your newly planted specimen will take many years to develop this sort of character, which will be something to celebrate, not hack at.

## Enjoy them...

When the fruit is completely ripe, in late August and early September, when it turns a deep red and becomes soft and juicy. If you can reach the fruit, it's best to hand pick if possible. The traditional way was to spread a clean sheet under the tree and give the branches a good shake. Eat the fruit immediately, preferably with cream.

## Look out for...

The juice staining your fingers, teeth and clothes. Mulberries are otherwise relatively trouble free.

## Worth trying...

'Chelsea' – A modern variety that starts cropping within a few years; the species, *Morus nigra*, can take 12 or more years.

Black mulberries look something like elongated blackberries but their flavour is altogether more special and they are very juicy.

**Don't forget**

A mulberry tree makes a splendid centrepiece in the centre of a lawn, but it can grow very large and the fruit may be difficult to harvest as a result. If grown as an espalier against a sunny wall, the fruit is considerably easier to pick.

# Nuts

The nuts that are most suitable for average gardens are hazels and their relations, as well as almonds, which need warm summers to produce crops. Almonds can also be trained as a fan against a warm wall, increasing the likelihood of crops (see pages 13–14). Larger gardens can cope with walnuts and sweet chestnuts, which eventually make very large trees, but there are also dwarf varieties, which are suitable for a smaller space. Restricting their roots slows growth.

## Cultivation

DIFFICULTY Easy; low input.

PLANT In deep, fertile but well-drained soil in a sunny, sheltered spot.

SPACE This depends on how you are growing them: give cobnuts and filberts 2.5–3m (8–10ft) and dwarf sweet chestnuts or dwarf walnuts 4.5–6m (15–20ft). Almonds need up to 4.5m (15ft), but are best fan-trained, when they take up less space. Hazels also need about 4.5m (15ft) but can be grown closer together, 1.2m (4ft) apart, as a shelter belt.

CARE Stake newly planted, single-stemmed trees for their first couple of years (see page 28), and keep them watered in dry spells for the first summer. Bushes are usually self-supporting. In mid- to late April, sprinkle a general-purpose feed over the soil underneath the entire canopy of branches (this coincides with the area taken up by the 'feeding' roots). Squirrels can be a problem once trees or bushes start carrying crops (see Look out for, opposite).

STORAGE Nuts keep for about six months in a cool, dry place. First, remove the fleshy outer skins of walnuts and the prickly cases from sweet chestnuts, and remove the leafy husks from cobnuts and filberts. Spread the nuts out in a shallow layer in a warm room to dry thoroughly; turn regularly.

## Keep them happy by...

Mulching with well-rotted organic matter or bark chippings every spring. This helps to retain moisture and suppress weeds, which would otherwise compete with the tree.

## Pruning

Compact varieties of walnuts and chestnuts shouldn't need pruning. Buy a well-shaped plant to begin with. A fan-trained almond will need regular attention to maintain its flat shape,

Almonds make an attractive addition to the fruit garden. The very hard shell that protects the nuts is covered in a felty skin.

Red filberts have many assets, not least their red-husked nuts. The catkins are long and red and the foliage is copper-coloured.

Sweet chestnuts are well protected in their spiny husks, but the battle to get them out is well worth it for the excellent flavour of the roasted nuts.

pruning from May through the summer (*see* pages 67–8). If you must prune a freestanding almond, do it in spring to avoid problems with disease. Hazels are usually left to their own devices, but can be coppiced for pea-sticks or bean-poles.

Cobnuts and filberts can be left alone when they are grown as ornamentals, but for good nut production it's worth pruning them. After planting, if the bush has a strong upright leader, remove its top at about 1.2m (4ft) to encourage lower branches. From then on, pruning aims to create a bushy tree on a short (60cm/2ft) trunk with an open centre – like a short-stemmed wine glass. Prune in late February each year, removing any stems in the centre to keep it open and shortening all the main branches by half, cutting just above an outward-facing bud. Suckers growing from the plant base (that is, on the short trunk) don't bear nuts, so cut them off.

## Enjoy them…

When they start falling from the trees in autumn (October to November), in the case of almonds, sweet chestnuts and walnuts. Hazels, cobnuts and filberts can be picked slightly green in September or October and eaten fresh. However, if you are planning to store them, wait until the shells are hard and brown before picking.

Walnuts are superior in every way, and being able to eat them fresh from the garden is a great treat. Recent research suggests walnut oil may be more beneficial to our health than olive oil.

## Restricting the roots

To restrict the roots of nuts you will need a large, fine-mesh bag, sold by specialist nurseries and mail-order organic gardening suppliers. Put the rootball into the bag before planting to control the root-spread of potentially large trees such as walnuts and sweet chestnuts. The netting allows the fine 'feeding' roots out, but imprisons the large roots. It's like growing the tree in a big tub, but without the bother of having to water it so much.

## Look out for…

Grey squirrels are a real pest and are very difficult to deter. Commercial animal-deterrent pepper powders, sprays and pellets are available, but they usually need reapplying frequently, especially after rain. Holes in shells and empty shells are usually the result of visits by boring bugs and weevils and there is no remedy.

## Worth trying…

**ALMOND** (*Prunus dulcis* var. *dulcis*)
Deciduous, flowering tree, grown as for peaches; best as fans on south-facing walls. Hand-pollinate if no bees are around (*see* box, page 37) and protect blossom from frosts on cold nights (*see* page 46). '**Mandaline**' is self-fertile and flowers in April after the worst of the frost is over. Harvest in early October.

**COBNUTS, HAZELNUTS AND FILBERTS** (*Corylus* species)
Deciduous shrubs with large, rounded leaves and long catkins. You need two different varieties to ensure pollination; if there are wild hazels growing near by you may get away with one.

**COBNUT** (*Corylus avellana*)
This is a large-fruited hazel. Good varieties include '**Cosford**' and '**Tonda di Giffoni**'.

**FILBERT** (*Corylus maxima*)
A close relative of the cobnut, but with shaggy husks that cover the nut; '**Kentish Cob**' and '**Merveille de Bollwiller**' (or '**Hall's Giant**') are reliable croppers.

**RED FILBERT** (*Corylus maxima* 'Purpurea')
An excellent dual-purpose nut bush with long red catkins on bare branches in spring, coppery-red foliage and a good crop of small nuts with frilly purple-red outer husks in autumn.

**HAZEL** (*Corylus avellana*)
Not highly productive, but has the benefit of also providing plant supports; will only fruit in years when it isn't coppiced.

**SWEET CHESTNUT** (*Castanea sativa*)
Deeply indented bark, jagged leaves and clusters of spiny nuts in October. Eventually becomes a huge tree. '**Regal**' is compact, reaching 4.5m (15ft) in ten years, and bears nuts within a few years of planting.

**WALNUT** (*Juglans regia*)
Craggy bark and attractive foliage but can reach 33m (100ft) high in time; '**Franquette**' is the choice for walnut-lovers with large gardens. Other named varieties, such as '**Broadview**', are generally smaller, and those grown by grafting will often start cropping within three or four years of planting instead of the traditional 10–15. Nuts are ready in October or November.

# Passionfruit

harvest **AUG, SEP, OCT**

Passionfruit is intriguing to grow and eat. It makes an attractive garden plant – even the decorative varieties often produce edible fruit – and the fruit is tantalizingly tropical in flavour, though pippy. The passionfruit sold in shops is the purple granadilla (*Passiflora edulis*), which is not as beautiful as some, but still quite attractive. For a combined decorative and fruiting plant, grow it on the patio; for bigger crops, grow it in a greenhouse or conservatory. It's easy to raise plants from seed and they'll start fruiting the following year.

## Cultivation

**DIFFICULTY** Easy; low input.

**SOW** Obtain seeds from specialist catalogues and sow two or three per small pot on a warm windowsill indoors in March/April. If three seedlings emerge, remove one. Pot up, as pairs, into larger containers as necessary without disturbing the roots.

**PLANT** Harden off the young plants gradually and plant outside in a well-prepared border against a south-facing wall in late May or early June. For indoor cultivation, plant in May in rich soil in a greenhouse or grow in a 38–45cm (15–18in) tub

Everything about passionfruit is exotic, from the oddly wrinkled, purple skin to the extremely fragrant and delicious, bright yellow flesh.

filled with John Innes No. 3 potting compost to which a little multipurpose compost and grit have been added. Provide netting, trellis or wigwams for them to climb on and tie in the existing stems. Tendrils will soon be produced and then the plants cling for themselves.

**SPACE** At least 2m (6ft) around the plant, with supports at the same height.

**CARE** Water well from May until September. Use liquid tomato feed once a week during this time. Plants in the open usually have no problems with pollination, but under cover, do it yourself (*see* box, page 37).

**STORAGE** They'll keep for a week in a fruit bowl.

## Keep them happy by…

Attending to watering, ensuring their climbing frame is an adequate size, and pruning properly in late winter.

## Pruning

In autumn, after the fruit has been picked, tidy plants but leave proper pruning until February. Cut back all the long, whippy growth made during the previous summer to within two buds of the main framework of permanent stems that are trained out over the wall or over the supports.

## Enjoy them…

As the fruit ripens to dark purple from late summer into autumn. Leave fruit on the plant until it starts to wrinkle slightly. Use secateurs to snip off individual fruits, complete with their own short stems.

## Look out for…

Generally trouble free, although the vines are prone to the usual pests when grown under glass, including whitefly, aphids and red spider mite (*see* pages 51–2). Aphids may also infect the plant with cucumber mosaic virus. There is no cure for this disease, which causes mottling in the leaves and reduced vigour. Dig up and destroy affected plants.

## Worth trying…

**'Crackerjack'** – Larger and more plentiful fruit; good for growing in pots on space-saving spirals or similar structures.

**Purple granadilla** (*Passiflora edulis*) – Large, glossy, three-lobed leaves up to 20cm (8in) long, and white flowers, followed by round, purple fruit, 5cm (2in) in diameter, with soft, juicy yellow flesh filled with dark seeds.

# Peaches and nectarines

### harvest JUL, AUG, SEP

Peaches and nectarines are a bit of a challenge to grow well, but they're worth the effort as there's little to beat the flavour of their fruit when it's picked straight off the tree. Even if crops aren't huge, the trees are attractive specimens with pink blossom on the bare branches in early spring; they're particularly lovely when fan-trained (*see* pages 13–14), which is the best way in our climate. However, if you don't have perfect growing conditions, you're wasting your time: the fruit either won't set, won't swell, or won't ripen; plant an apricot instead.

## Cultivation

DIFFICULTY Intermediate; moderate input (nectarines are shorter-lived and harder to grow than peaches).
PLANT Fan-train the trees against a sunny, south-facing wall or fence (*see* pages 67–8), or along a post-and-wire support in a sheltered situation (*see* pages 30–1). The soil needs to be rich, fertile and well drained. Prepare a bed especially for the trees at the base of the wall and work plenty of well-rotted organic matter into the soil.
SPACE Provide a wall or fence 1.5–2m (5–6ft) high and up to 2.5m (8ft) wide.
CARE Mulch generously every spring, and in mid- to late April feed with general-purpose fertilizer. Water in dry spells, especially when the tree is carrying fruit. For best results hand-pollinate (*see* page 37), and if a frost or cold, windy weather is predicted while the plants are in flower, cover them with fleece (*see* page 46). Keep a watch on the fruit from early July onwards, and once the first ones start colouring up, cover the plant with netting to protect from birds (*see* pages 46–7).
STORAGE You can preserve them and make pies, but they really are best eaten straight from the tree.

## Keep them happy by...

Providing a really sheltered, sunny site – it's the best way to ensure success. If you have the choice, planting trees in an enclosed area such as a courtyard is best, since it provides protection against wind, will radiate heat and help to ripen the fruit. Red brick walls are particularly good at retaining heat.

'Peregrine' is a deservedly popular peach variety producing red-flushed, creamy white-skinned fruit with delicious white flesh. If it likes your conditions, it will crop well.

## Pot-grown peaches and nectarines

Dwarf peaches and nectarines are perfect for growing in pots in a sheltered, sunny position. Several varieties are available, but many are simply sold as 'patio peach' or 'patio nectarine'. They are genetic dwarfs that are very slow-growing (to 1.2m/4ft after ten years).

Buy a tree in spring and repot it into a 38–45cm (15–18in) tub with plenty of drainage material in the bottom, and filled with John Innes No. 3 potting compost – add to this 10 per cent each of multipurpose compost and potting grit, which makes the mixture crumbly and free-draining. Provide a stake for support (*see* page 35). Protect the flowers from frost and bad weather with fleece. If you have a greenhouse, consider bringing the pots under cover during flowering. Water regularly in the growing season and also very dry spells in winter. Use liquid tomato feed every week from late April to the end of August.

The flowers of nectarine 'Lord Napier' brighten up the garden in early spring, but it is the juicy, dark crimson fruit that make it popular with fruit gardeners.

Often sold under names such as 'patio nectarine', dwarf nectarines are excellent for growing in containers. Position them near a sunny, sheltered wall to protect the flowers in spring and ripen the fruit later on.

## Pruning

With fan-trained trees, follow the techniques for fan-training fruit trees (*see* pages 67–8). Trim container plants only when necessary to maintain their shape.

## Enjoy them…

From late July to early September, depending on the variety. Leave the fruit on the tree until it is completely ripe: ripe fruit gradually develops a warm pink or red flush, and feels slightly soft to the touch; it often has a faint scent too. Once the first fruits start ripening, check the tree daily and pick any as they reach perfection. If allowed to overripen they will fall off and spoil. The total crop will usually ripen over a period of three or four weeks.

## Look out for…

Peach leaf curl is the most serious disease of peaches and nectarines, and most plants grown in the open get it at some time. Greenhouse-grown plants are seldom affected. Large red-blistered areas appear on the foliage in summer; these are followed by white, powdery spores and then the leaves drop prematurely. Affected trees are badly weakened and cropping is inevitably reduced. Spray trees thoroughly with copper-based fungicide twice, at ten-day intervals in February, and repeat in autumn just before the leaves start to drop. Rake up fallen leaves and burn them. Spraying with foliar feed will often help the plants to recover.

Patches of gum on the bark may be caused by poor cultivation techniques (*see* Apricots, page 79).

## Worth trying…

**'Duke of York'** – Pale yellow-fleshed peaches are ripe in mid-July.

**'Lord Napier'** – White-fleshed nectarine with a great flavour. Ripens in early August. Probably the best nectarine variety for growing outside.

**'Peregrine'** – Reliable, white-fleshed peach ripening mid- to late August.

**'Rochester'** – Yellow-fleshed peach ripening in early August. Very reliable.

# Pears

## harvest SEP, OCT

Unlike their close relations the apples, pears can be tricky to grow and are relatively slow to come to fruit. They're generally sensitive to cold weather and are quite fussy about soil and like to have a regular supply of water. Also, when it comes to harvesting you need to pick, store and ripen in three distinct stages for best results. On the plus side, they suffer fewer pests and diseases than apples. And, there are all those wonderful varieties with their delicious names to choose from, such as 'Doyenné du Comice' and 'Beurré Superfin'.

## Cultivation

DIFFICULTY Challenging; moderate to high input.
PLANT For anything other than 'Conference' you'll need a warm, sunny, sheltered spot with fertile, well-drained soil. Increase your chances by growing them as espaliers (*see* pages 11, 14 and 65) or single or double cordons against a south-facing wall (*see* pages 13–14).

SPACE Freestanding trees on Quince A rootstocks (*see* page 15) should be spaced 4.5m (15ft) apart, those on Quince C rootstocks can be 3m (10ft) apart. Plant espaliers 2.5–3m (8–10ft) apart, single cordons 75cm (30in) apart and double cordons 1.5m (5ft) apart.
CARE Keep newly planted trees watered in dry spells for their first summer. Each spring mulch generously and in mid- to late April feed with general-purpose fertilizer. In a dry summer, water trees while they are carrying a crop of fruit, especially those against a wall or fence, which suffer more from drought.
STORAGE Pears need to be stored before they are ready to eat. Store them under cover in a cool place, such as a shed or garage; bring them in a few at a time as they reach their peak time (*see* page 106, Worth trying) – they'll ripen within a few days. Don't bring pears straight indoors from the garden: late pears in particular will either stay rock hard or turn 'sleepy' (brown and mealy-textured inside).

## Keep them happy by...

Providing a suitable pollinating partner (*see* page 19). Even self-fertile varieties crop far better when cross-pollinated. If you are

'Onward' is a relative newcomer that, like its parent 'Doyenné du Comice', is extremely delicious and also a reliable cropper. It is ready to eat in early autumn.

'Conference' pears are the easiest variety to grow and have been the home-grown pear of choice for many years. They have juicy, firm flesh that makes them excellent for cooking.

If you grow 'Doyenné du Comice' you have to accept that the crop won't necessarily be huge, but what you do get will be worth its weight in gold as far as flavour goes.

short of space, it's well worth planting a family pear tree for more reliable results. This consists of branches of several different varieties grafted onto a single trunk, so a single tree produces three different types of pear. They are selected to be pollinating partners, too, such as 'Conference', 'Doyenné du Comice' and 'Williams' Bon Chrétien'.

## Pruning

Prune freestanding standard pear trees in winter in the same way as for apples (see pages 76–8), and prune cordons, stepovers or each 'arm' of an espalier in late July (see pages 64–6).

## Enjoy them…

From September onwards, although some late varieties hang on until mid-October. Harvesting is tricky: you need to pick the pears at exactly the right moment and bring them in to finish them off, and it's not easy to recognize this moment. Don't leave them on the trees to ripen fully as this makes them go 'sleepy'. Visually, there is little warning; there is only a minor colour change, the skin turning very slightly lighter, and some varieties may develop a faint warm flush, but you might get a hint by the first windfalls. Test your hunch by lifting a pear in a cupped hand; if it lifts off the tree complete with its stalk, it's ready, otherwise leave it slightly longer. Check them constantly, especially if bad weather is forecast, otherwise they may be knocked off the trees and spoiled.

'Williams' Bon Chrétien' are plump, soft, sweet and juicy dessert pears. The skin is green, faintly marked with red. Pick in early September and use throughout the month.

## Look out for…

Scab, a fungal disease, causes black or brown cracks with corky edges on the fruit, which can be misshapen, and khaki blotches on the leaves, plus premature leaf fall (see Apples, page 76).

Pear leaf blister mite can affect pears grown against walls. The leaves develop yellow or red blisters that eventually turn black. Pick off and burn leaves when you spot a problem.

Pear midges are grubs that roll up the leaves. Pick off and burn affected leaves.

Small, stunted fruits are due to poor growing conditions or poor pollination. Feed and mulch the tree very well each spring and make it more comfortable, perhaps by covering it with fleece on cold nights around flowering time. Plant a pollinator (see page 19) – 'Conference' or 'Concorde' are safe bets even if you don't know the name of your own variety. Above all, guard against poor, dry soil. On chalky soil they can sometimes suffer from iron deficiency, so feed with sequestered iron.

As with apples, fireblight can also cause problems for pears (see pages 52 and 78).

## Worth trying…

'Beurré Superfin' – Yellow, slightly russeted skin and sweet, juicy flesh; 'Conference'-shaped fruit. Pick September; ready October – the fruit does not keep for long. 'Conference' is a suitable pollinator.

'Concorde' ('Conference' x 'Doyenné du Comice') – Reliable and easy with light green fruit with faint brown russeting. Pick September; use October and November. Self-fertile; a good pollinator of many varieties.

'Conference' – Elongated, greeny-brown fruit, for eating and cooking; very reliable and heavy cropping. Pick September; use October and November. Not self-fertile, as is often suggested, but usually manages to crop well even if it is the only pear in the immediate locality. It is a good pollinator for many varieties.

'Doyenné du Comice' – A large, fat dessert pear with pale green skin heavily covered with brown russeting and faint red 'cheeks'. It has very rich, juicy, melting flesh. Pick mid-October; use November and December. 'Conference' is a good pollinator.

'Onward' – Similar to 'Doyenné du Comice', but ready earlier. Pick in mid-September; use in late September. Does not keep. 'Concorde' is a suitable pollinating partner.

'Red Williams' – Similar to 'Doyenné du Comice' but with red-skinned fruit when ripe. Pick from late August; use throughout September. Cross-pollinated by 'Conference'.

'Williams' Bon Chrétien' (see left).

# Plums, damsons and greengages

Plums and their relatives are very widely grown and successful garden fruits. The fruit is often abundant and the trees themselves are easy to cultivate. Plums are mostly grown as freestanding trees, but fan-trained plums or cordons are occasionally available. Although many plums are not self-fertile, there is often another plum in the neighbourhood, so pollinating partners (*see* page 19) are not always necessary. The plum family includes wonderful old-fashioned fruit such as greengages, damsons, mirabelles and those hedgerow-dwellers sloes and bullaces. Many were great favourites in cottage gardens.

## Cultivation

**DIFFICULTY** Easy; low input.
**PLANT** In a sheltered, sunny spot in fertile, well-drained soil.
**SPACE** A freestanding tree on Pixy (*see* page 15) will need 4.5m (15ft) of space; allow a run of 3.6m (12ft) for a fan-trained tree.
**CARE** Keep new plants watered in dry spells for their first summer. Mulch generously each spring and in April sprinkle a double handful of general-purpose fertilizer over the soil beneath each tree. Thin fruit if necessary (*see* below and page 73). As fruits begin ripening, protect a fan-trained plum from birds by draping it with netting, although birds are less of a problem with plums than with other fruit.
**STORAGE** Make jams and jellies or pies. You can also freeze plums, but remove the stones first.

## Keep them happy by...

Thinning out a heavy crop once it has set – the plums will be green and half-size. 'Victoria' in particular is renowned for cropping very heavily every other year and taking a year off in between to recover, and crop-thinning helps to prevent this. It also avoids the branches snapping under the weight of the fruit. Snip fruit off at the stalk with secateurs, leaving the biggest and best 5–8cm (2–3in) apart along the branches.

## Pruning

Avoid pruning plums and damsons. Choose a well-shaped tree with four or five strong branches round the top of the trunk. Remove any damaged branches during the growing season in late spring or summer. For information on fan-training plum trees, *see* pages 67–8.

## Enjoy them...

In summer and autumn, as soon as the first few ripe windfalls begin to drop. When harvesting, choose well-coloured fruits that are soft and drop into your hands with a gentle pull. Leave plum stalks on the branch and keep the stalk on the fruit for damsons and greengages. Depending on the variety, you could be picking plums and greengages from late July to the end of September and damsons in September and October.

Aside from apple varieties, 'Victoria' plum must be one of the best-known names of any fruit. It is very widely grown and famous for producing branch-snappingly heavy crops.

## Look out for...

Little or no fruit may be due to a lack of a suitable pollinator (even so-called self-fertile varieties produce bigger and better crops if there's a pollinator near by), or biennial bearing caused by allowing a heavy cropper to carry enormous crops without thinning.

If the leaves take on a silvery sheen, turn brown and die, your plum has silver leaf disease (*see* page 53).

Gummy lumps appearing on otherwise healthy bark may be caused by stress or poor cultivation techniques (*see* Apricots, page 79).

## Worth trying...

**'Czar'** – Heavy crops of medium-sized, oval, purple fruit; for cooking. Self-fertile. Ripens in early August.

**'Marjorie's Seedling'** – One of the very best cooking plums, but also good for eating, with large, oval, purple-skinned fruit. Self-fertile. Ripens in late September and early October.

**'Merryweather'** – A damson with large, round, purple fruit. Self-fertile. Ripens in September.

**Myrobalan** or **cherry plum** (*Prunus cerasifera*) – Very small, round plums that look like cherries. Self-fertile, and ripens in late July. There are also named hybrids with red or yellow fruit. They cross-pollinate each other, but are also pollinated by 'Victoria' (*see* page 107 and below).

**'Old Green Gage'** – Small, flavoursome, yellowy-green gages, but rather light and irregular crops; ripens late August/early September. Pollinated by 'Marjorie's Seedling'.

**'Ouillin's Golden Gage'** – Heavy crops of tasty dessert fruits ripening in early August from pale green to red-streaked gold. A gage-like plum that could almost be mistaken for an apricot. Pollinated by 'Victoria'.

**'Victoria'** – This heavy-cropping, firm favourite is a dessert plum but is also used for cooking. It has large, oval, very sweet, juicy fruit; rich red, flushed pale gold and darker red. Ripens from the end of August into September, slightly earlier in a hot summer. If you can grow only one, it is likely to be 'Victoria' – the perfect dual-purpose 'lone' plum tree.

Damsons make the most beautiful jam – dark, rich, fragrant and not too sweet, just like the fruit themselves.

'Ouillin's Golden Gage' is a plum with scented fruit that ripens to a rich gold with red tinges and streaks. It is excellent for eating either fresh or cooked. It flowers later than most.

### Don't forget

Avoid pruning plum and damson trees unless absolutely necessary. If you must prune, do so in late spring or summer, to reduce the chance of infection from silver leaf disease.

# Quinces and medlars

harvest OCT

The true edible quince is *Cydonia oblonga*, an attractive, medium-sized tree with very large white or pale pink blossom in spring, followed by pear-like fruit in autumn. It's pretty enough to grow as a decorative tree in the lawn or at the back of a border. Quinces are too hard and sour to eat raw but they are excellent in cooking, for quince jelly or in pies, crumbles and tarts. They impart a rich, aromatic flavour. Medlars are also decorative with good autumn foliage on a small to medium-sized tree. The fruits are about 4cm (1¾in) across and look rather like carved Tudor roses. They are eaten after they have gone rotten ('bletted').

## Cultivation

**DIFFICULTY** Very easy; low input.
**PLANT** In deep, rich, fertile, well-drained soil, in a sheltered, sunny site in a reasonably mild location.
**SPACE** Allow for the tree to grow 4.5m (15ft) high and wide.
**CARE** Stake a new tree for two or three years, but once established it does not need support. Keep a newly planted tree watered in dry spells for its first summer. Mulch generously each spring, and in April sprinkle a general-purpose fertilizer underneath the entire canopy.
**STORAGE** Quinces keep for several weeks in a cool, dry place. Medlars must be allowed to rot. Both can be kept long term, used for jellies or frozen in pies and other dishes.

## Keep them happy by...
Giving them plenty of space all around for even growth.

## Pruning
No regular pruning is necessary, except the removal of dead, diseased or unwanted stems in winter.

## Enjoy them...
Quinces are ready to pick when they lift easily off the tree in your hand, without pulling or twisting. However, if October brings windy weather and they are not properly ripe, cut the remaining fruits, complete with stalks, using secateurs and bring them indoors to finish ripening. Even when they are fully ripe, they are still very hard. Remove the pips, as they are toxic. Ripe quinces have a wonderful perfume.

Harvest medlars in mid- to late October, shortly after the leaves fall from the tree. Keep the clean, dry fruits in a shed for a few weeks (spread out in trays) until they start to soften.

## Look out for...
Fireblight may strike (*see* page 52 and Apples, page 78).

## Worth trying...
'**Nottingham**' – The medlar that is most often offered for sale.
'**Vranja**' – A quince with large, pink, pear-like blossom in spring, followed by enormous crops of pale green, felty-textured, pear-like fruit that becomes very large, fragrant and pale golden and ripens in October. Self-fertile and very reliable.
'**Meech's Prolific**' is similar to 'Vranja'.

The fruit of the quince is intriguing and beautiful with a most tempting perfume, but don't try it raw as it is also rock hard and very sour.

Medlars are an oddity in that they are eaten when they are more or less rotten. This is perhaps why they are traditionally consumed with cheese and a glass of port.

# Raspberries

If you're wondering whether it's worth the trouble to grow your own fruit, allow raspberries to help you make up your mind: they are perfect eaten with cream, ice cream, in fruit salads and in a wide variety of other summery puddings. They also make good, if pippy, jam. Shop-bought raspberries are often tasteless and a bit solid in texture (or squishy and overripe) and they're also expensive. If you grow a selection of your own, you can pick them when they become ripe and enjoy them through summer and into autumn, for next to nothing.

## Cultivation

DIFFICULTY Easy; moderate input.
PLANT In good, fertile, well-drained, neutral or slightly acid soil full of well-rotted organic matter. The canes need a sheltered spot that gets the sun for half the day at least.
SPACE Plants 45cm (18in) apart. Rows should be 2m (6ft) apart for summer-fruiting varieties, 90cm (3ft) for autumn varieties, which are shorter. Provide adequate support (see pages 30–1).
CARE In spring, sprinkle general-purpose fertilizer along each side of the row and mulch the plants heavily with well-rotted organic matter. Water during dry spells through summer and into autumn. It's best not to allow autumn-fruiting raspberries to fruit in the first year as this enables them to establish better.
STORAGE Raspberries are best eaten fresh, but small, slightly underripe berries can be frozen.

## Keep them happy by…

Making sure they get plenty of water while they're carrying a crop, otherwise you'll get fewer, small, hard fruit.

## Training and pruning

After planting, remove any thin, weak or distorted shoots and loosely tie the rest to the support. As the canes grow, tie them to the support wires. If the canes grow much taller than the top wire, cut them off 15cm (6in) above it.

Summer-fruiting raspberries fruit on canes produced the previous year, so the idea behind pruning is to remove these after they have fruited (they won't fruit again) and to encourage a healthy number of new canes that will then supply next year's fruits (see below).

Autumn-fruiting raspberries bear their crop on the new canes, so the aim of pruning is to produce plenty of strong, healthy new canes (see opposite). You can also get a crop in summer by leaving about a quarter of the old canes in place

Summer-fruiting raspberries are easy to care for with very little in the way of pruning necessary. 'Leo' (left) is relatively late to ripen and has a good flavour.

### Don't forget

Ideally, in order to prevent possible diseases from taking hold, avoid planting new canes where raspberries have been grown in the previous seven years or so.

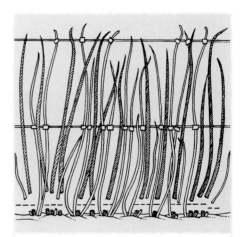

After summer-fruiting raspberries have fruited, remove the old canes and cut weak new ones down to soil level. Tie in strong new shoots, spacing them evenly along the support. After leaf fall, reduce tall canes to 15cm (6in) above the top wire.

when you prune. These canes will crop in summer while still allowing new ones to grow and crop in autumn.

## Enjoy them...

Fully ripe by leaving them on the canes until a day or two after they have turned red (or yellow). Give the fruit a gentle pull between thumb and forefinger; if it doesn't come away, leaving the plug on the plant, it isn't ready – give it another day. The fruit ripens from late June into August, and as late as November in a good year (frosts put paid to the fruit).

## Look out for...

Birds love raspberries and will eat even unripe fruit, so cover rows with netting as soon as the first few berries start turning pink (see pages 46–7).

Several viruses affect raspberries, stunting the plants and reducing the yield; they also cause yellow blotches or mottling on the foliage. Viruses are common, spread by greenfly, and they affect other cane fruit as well. There is no cure, just dig up and destroy affected canes. Replace old plants after ten years in any case, as they will have much reduced in vigour by then. Plant the next lot in a new patch of ground.

Yellowing leaves, stunted growth and poor yield usually point to lime-induced chlorosis (a result of an over-alkaline soil). If growing raspberries in even slightly alkaline soil, apply sulphur powder or sulphur chips to the ground in spring (available from some garden centres but mainly from specialist suppliers), or use a chelated iron feed (sequestrene) of the sort used for rhododendrons and camellias. Repeat this treatment each year, in early spring.

Cane blight and cane spot are two serious diseases producing black-based or purple-spotted canes. There is no cure, although fungicides may keep cane spot under control. It is better to destroy affected plants, plant new plants in fresh ground, or grow a resistant variety to begin with.

Fruit that is dry and brown at the stalk end may contain the larvae of raspberry beetles. There is no treatment, but if you spot the egg-laying adults, which are

4mm (less than ¼in) long and brown, it is best to squash them immediately. Autumn fruit is less likely to be affected.

## Worth trying...

'**All Gold**' – Autumn-fruiting with well-flavoured, yellow fruit.
'**Autumn Bliss**' – Autumn-fruiting with tasty, medium-sized red fruit from mid-August. Does not need supporting.
'**Glen Ample**' – Summer-fruiting raspberry ripening from late June. Spine-free.
'**Leo**' – Summer-fruiting with tangy red fruit from late July. Disease-resistant.
'**Malling Admiral**' – Summer-fruiting raspberry ripening from mid-July. Good disease resistance and spineless.
'**Malling Jewel**' – Summer-fruiting raspberry ripening in early July; excellent flavour. Good resistance to virus.

### The lazy way to grow autumn-fruiting raspberries

Follow the pruning regime described below, but if the canes are not too crowded leave them as they are, without thinning. The result will be a thick hedge of canes about 30cm (12in) wide. After a few years you will need to thin, but until then you should get enormous crops of fruit from a very limited space, provided you feed and mulch generously.

### HOW TO prune and train autumn-fruiting raspberries

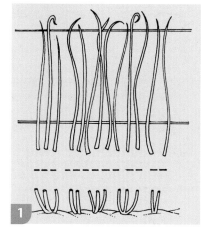

**1** In late winter or just before bud burst, cut all raspberry canes to 8cm (3in) above ground level. Alternatively, you could leave a few canes on the plant for some summer fruits.

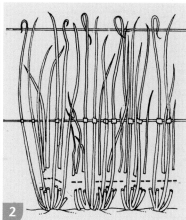

**2** In early summer, thin out the new shoots to 8–10cm (3–4in) apart. Remove any surplus canes to avoid overcrowding, and take out all shoots less than 1m (40in) high. Tie in the remaining new shoots.

# Red and whitecurrants

**harvest** JUL, AUG

Not many people would eat redcurrants on their own, but they do make a wonderful addition to other fruit dishes, such as summer puddings, fruit fools and pies, and they go especially well with raspberries. Redcurrant jelly is good too. The plants look attractive when in fruit, with their long tassels (trusses) of brilliant scarlet currants; they are especially eye-catching trained as U-shaped double cordons against a wall (*see* pages 16–17). Whitecurrants are the same shape and size as redcurrants, but taste sweeter and ripen to warm cream-buff. They are grown in the same way.

## Cultivation

**DIFFICULTY** Easy; low input.
**PLANT** In a sheltered situation in fertile, well-drained soil. Redcurrants can cope in a slightly shady area, but are happier in a sunnier spot – where the fruit ripens earlier and tastes sweeter.
**SPACE** Bushes 1.2–1.5m (4–5ft) apart; plant double cordons 60cm (2ft) apart.
**CARE** Mulch in spring and sprinkle general-purpose fertilizer around the plants in April. Water the bushes generously during dry spells in summer.
**STORAGE** Eat fresh if possible. If necessary, preserve in pies and puddings.

## Keep them happy by...

Watering well when the weather is dry, especially while they are carrying a crop, otherwise the fruit will be small and sparse – in a very dry year it may fail completely.

## Pruning

Like gooseberries, redcurrants are grown on a short trunk or 'leg' (*see* page 70). Prune redcurrant bushes from November to February, as with gooseberry bushes, and train and prune double cordons in late June or early July.

## Enjoy them...

In mid- and late summer, when the fruits increase in size and turn a brighter red or a richer creamy buff. Pick before the first fruits become overripe, otherwise they start to fall off the plant. Take the entire truss of fruit by tearing it gently from the plant with an upward movement of your hand.

Redcurrant 'Red Lake' has fruit like delicate jewels, hanging seductively beneath the pale green leaves. Maybe too seductive – if unprotected, your crop will go to the birds.

## Look out for...

Large red blisters might appear on leaves in summer and are caused by the redcurrant blister aphid. On whitecurrants and blackcurrants it causes yellow blisters. The aphids are pale yellow – look under the leaves in spring and early summer. Check plants regularly and spray with an organic remedy if an outbreak is seen. Alternatively, in late June, cut the tips of the sideshoots back almost as far as the first fruits. This removes the blistering and increases light and air to the ripening fruit, besides keeping the plants in check.

Sawfly larvae can infest the leaves (*see* Gooseberries, page 91). Coral spot causes dieback in affected shoots, which then develop orange-pink spots. Remove all affected shoots, cutting back into healthy bark. Burn all prunings.

## Worth trying...

'**Blanka**' – Very heavy-cropping whitecurrant ripening in late July and August.
'**Jonkheer van Tets**' – Redcurrant with long trusses of large berries (so less fiddly to pick) in early July.
'**Red Lake**' – Redcurrant with large crops of juicy berries on long trusses in early July.
'**Stanza**' – Small, dark red currants in late July and August. The flowers open late, so are not affected by late frosts.
'**White Versailles**' – Whitecurrant with large, sweet fruit ripening in July.

# Rhubarb

**harvest**  MAR, APR, MAY, JUN, JUL

Even though it's not strictly a fruit, rhubarb should have a place in everyone's fruit garden. It is tasty and versatile, making the best pies and crumbles you're ever likely to eat, and it's good for you too. Its only drawback is that you usually do need to use sugar on it. Forced rhubarb (*see* box) is a delicacy, since forcing makes the stems grow earlier, more slender and very succulent.

## Cultivation

**DIFFICULTY** Easy; low input.

**PLANT** In very heavily manured, reasonably heavy soil; if you can, put it near the compost heap where it will enjoy the rich runoff in the soil. Give it full sun so the stems will develop a redder colour and a sweeter, richer flavour. To create new plants, divide the rootball and replant the pieces (*see* page 44).

**SPACE** Allow 90cm (3ft) around each plant.

**CARE** Water well, particularly if you plant pot-grown specimens in the middle of the growing season. Remove flowering stems in summer. Cut them out as close to the base as you can without harming the plant. Every autumn as the foliage dies down, remove the dead leaves, sprinkle general-purpose fertilizer all round the plants and mulch.

**STORAGE** Rhubarb must be cooked before eating, but can be frozen either raw or cooked.

## Keep them happy by…

Mulching at least once a year with well-rotted manure. The next best thing is garden compost.

## Enjoy them…

As and when you want to between March and July, but then allow the plant to grow naturally for the rest of the season so it recovers. Choose well-coloured stems whose leaves have just opened out fully, as these are the most tasty and tender. Don't cut the stems: hold the stalk firmly near the base and tug and twist so it comes out cleanly, including the bit that clasps round the top of the root. Trim this and the leaves before cooking.

## Look out for…

Dull, listless foliage, small, sickly stems and the growth buds dying off are symptoms of crown rot. There is no cure; remove and destroy affected plants and plant new ones in a different spot.

Although 'Timperley Early' is widely appreciated by fruit gardeners as a very early, forcing rhubarb, this variety can also be enjoyed as a normal crop later in the year. It has very thin, red and green stems.

### Don't forget

Rhubarb leaves are poisonous, so remove them before cooking and handle them with care. Despite their toxicity, the leaves can still be used on the compost heap.

### Forcing rhubarb

Any well-established rhubarb can be encouraged to produce some very early, thin, blanched stems. Cover the crown with a rhubarb forcing pot, or an upturned dustbin or similar large container in mid-January or early February. Ideally, put straw around the pot for insulation. Within a few weeks, long stems with pale yellowy-coloured leaves appear. Pull as many of these as you want until the end of March, but then uncover the plant and allow it to grow naturally, taking only a small crop of stems for the rest of that season. Rhubarb is quite resilient and if you mulch and feed them properly in autumn, the crowns can take this treatment every year, but if you have two crowns, be kind and alternate them.

## Worth trying…

**'Hawke's Champagne'** (or 'Champagne') – Excellent flavour with thick, heavily red-flushed green stems. Harvest in spring and early summer.

**'Stockbridge Arrow'** – Very tasty with thick, rich pink-red stems. This is a very early variety that is bred especially for forcing in heat but it can also be cultivated in the conventional way.

**'Timperley Early'** – A very early variety; when forced, it will crop from February onwards; you can often pick a few slender stems as late as July or August too.

# Strawberries

**harvest** JUN, JUL, AUG, SEP, OCT

Once you've tasted home-grown strawberries, you'll never want to eat any other kind. They smell wonderful and are brightly coloured, soft, juicy and full of flavour. The other benefits are that you can grow a selection of varieties that ripen at different times, taste different and have fruit of varying sizes. Each plant yields roughly 225g (8oz) of fruit, so plant enough for your needs.

## Cultivation

**DIFFICULTY** Reasonably easy; moderate input.
**PLANT** Ideally, put in young plants in August or September so they're well established for cropping the following summer; alternatively, plant in late autumn or early spring and put up with a smaller first-year crop. Choose a sunny, sheltered spot with humus-rich, fertile, well-drained soil. Avoid planting strawberries where you've grown potatoes, tomatoes or chrysanthemums; all these plants are prone to verticillium wilt, which can kill the fruit. Strawberries also grow very well in containers (*see* pages 16, 20 and 32–4).
**SPACE** Where possible, space each plant 45cm (18in) apart in rows 90cm (3ft) apart. In a raised bed with deep, rich soil you can grow 30–38cm (12–15in) apart with 60cm (2ft) between rows.
**CARE** In early spring apply 15g (½oz) of sulphate of potash per square metre (square yard) of strawberry bed, sprinkling it carefully between the plants. In early summer, as the first small green fruits appear, spread straw or lay synthetic strawberry mats between the plants (*see* page 40). Tuck these under the

'Florence' is a good choice if you want some strawberries later in the year. Water carefully and regularly while the fruits are developing to ensure plenty of large berries.

foliage and around the 'collar' of the plants to smother weeds and protect the fruit from splashes, which make them dirty and damp. Water carefully between the plants, as splashed strawberries often turn mouldy.

Protect the plants from birds, either inside a fruit cage or with netting (*see* pages 46–7). After the whole crop has been picked, clip strawberry plants over with a pair of shears to remove all the old fruit stems, leaves and runners, and finally feed the bed with a general-purpose fertilizer and water it in well. The plants soon make healthy, fresh new growth that sets them up for cropping well again next year. Strawberry plants crop well for three or four years, after which they are best replaced with new young plants.
**STORAGE** Strawberries should be eaten straight from the garden, but a glut will make good jam.

## Keep them happy by…

Watering and weeding well. Being shallow-rooted, strawberries are the first fruits to suffer from dry weather and they are quickly overrun by weeds, so pay particular attention to regular weeding, and water them thoroughly in dry spells.

## Enjoy them…

When perfectly ripe. Once the strawberries have turned red, give them a couple more days to fatten up and really ripen. Pick over plants daily, and don't leave small or misshapen ones behind, since they'll go mouldy and may spread disease. Use them in cooking or jam instead.

## Look out for…

Slugs and snails are the bane of the strawberry grower. It is never too early to begin the war against them. Keep weeds down and clear any debris under which they might hide. In raised beds with wooden edges, consider using copper strips (available from organic supplies catalogues). You tack the strip along the edge of the bed and this gives the slugs a mild electric shock, which deters them from venturing further.

Grey mould, or botrytis (*see* page 52), can affect strawberries. It is worse in damp summers or if the fruit is splashed when you're watering. Keep weeds controlled and space plants fairly well apart to improve air circulation; avoid spraying with fungicide, particularly if you want to use the fruit in preserves. (It's usually too late by the time fruit is going mouldy anyway.)

Yellow, blotchy leaves and progressively low yields are due to strawberry virus, particularly if the plants are several years old or you propagate your own replacement plants from runners. The virus is spread by greenfly, so you'll usually get it eventually. Dig out and destroy affected plants as soon as you see the problem, before it can be spread to the others, and buy virus-free stock to start a new row at the first opportunity. Zap greenfly to prevent them spreading the disease in the first place.

Verticillium wilt is often fatal. It makes the leaves wilt then turn brown. There is no cure, so remove affected plants, and surrounding soil if possible, as soon as you spot a problem.

Red core is a disease of heavy or damp soils. It stunts the plants, which grow reddish leaves and may collapse. If you have this problem, destroy your current plants, change the site, and improve your drainage.

## Worth trying...

'**Cambridge Favourite**' – Medium-sized, tasty fruit from late June to late July; produces heavy crops on easily grown, disease-resistant plants.

'**Cambridge Late Pine**' – Wonderful flavour from dark red, beautifully fragrant fruit; ripens mid-June to mid-July. Sadly, low yields and low disease resistance; can be difficult to obtain.

'**Elsanta**' – Large crops of well-flavoured berries; mid-June to mid-July. Very reliable – a good beginner's variety.

'**Flamenco**' – A so-called 'perpetual fruiter', with heavy crops of deliciously flavoured fruit in flushes from late August until autumn frosts.

'**Florence**' – Late cropper with large, firm fruit ripening from

### Alpine strawberries

These are dwarf plants producing tiny fruit that is sweet and bursting with flavour. The plants are grown from seed as they don't produce runners. Sow in early spring under glass or on a bright but not hot windowsill indoors, and prick out the seedlings into 8cm (3in) pots when large enough to handle. Plant out the young plants 23cm (9in) apart in summer. You might get some fruit the same summer, but the following couple of years will be the most productive.

early July to early August. Good disease resistance.

'**Honeoye**' – Good flavour, medium-sized fruit throughout June. Some grey mould resistance.

'**Mae**' – Grown for its early fruiting abilities – mid- to late May if protected with cloches in spring, otherwise ready in June and early July.

'**Mara des Bois**' – A 'perpetual fruiter' with a lovely flavour of wild strawberries; fruits from late summer into autumn.

'**Pegasus**' – Sweet-flavoured, medium to large strawberries towards the end of June. Disease-resistant.

'**Royal Sovereign**' – An old favourite that can't quite compete with modern varieties, but has an outstanding flavour. Light crops of small fruit in early June to mid-July. If you choose to grow it, be prepared to pamper it.

## HOW TO propagate using runners

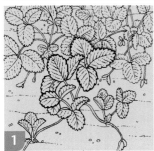

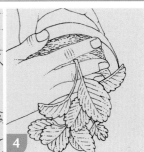

In the growing season, plants produce several long, thin stems (known as runners), each with several small plantlets attached. Select three or four runners to propagate on each plant.

Fill pots with multipurpose compost. Bury each pot in the soil beside the plant and position a plantlet in it. Use a piece of bent wire to hold it in place.

After a few weeks, the plantlet will have formed roots and will be growing away. In the autumn, detach it from the parent plant by cutting cleanly through the runner.

Leave the young plant in the pot to grow a healthy set of roots. Plant it out in the strawberry bed or in a container in the usual way the following spring (see pages 29 and 33).

# Season by season

One of the most challenging things about gardening is getting all the jobs done when they need doing. If you're busy with other things at work or with the family, it's so easy to forget or to delay. Although in many cases being a bit early or late is not a problem, there are times when it's important to plant, prune or thin, or harvest fruit within a certain period. Here is an overview of each of the four seasons, outlining the tasks that need doing to ensure you have healthy plants and a productive and tidy fruit garden.

# The fruit gardening year

From the north of Scotland to the south of England, the British Isles experience a wide range of weather conditions throughout the year. Winters are longer and colder in the north and shorter and warmer in the south. This means that when southerners are enjoying early spring, northerners are still shivering through late winter. It also makes it impossible to generalize about when plants will flower, or when fruit will be ready to harvest. However, gardeners need schedules, and the calendar months are a convenient way to indicate when particular things might happen and when various jobs should be done. For the purposes of this book, I've assumed that spring starts in March, summer in June, autumn in September and winter in December. Take this as a starting point and then move dates forwards or backwards, making adjustments depending on what you know happens where you live.

You can rely on a 'Victoria' plum tree to produce a satisfyingly large crop of sweet, fragrant and juicy fruit.

## The autumn season

The best time to plant a fruit garden is the autumn. Pot-grown fruit planted now will have a chance to establish before the onset of the winter weather, and by spring will feel quite at home in their new surroundings. Late autumn to early spring is when nurseries sell bare-rooted specimens, which is the traditional way of buying fruit trees, and the only way to buy certain varieties, as well as the most economical. Put in your order early, as the more unusual ones will sell out.

Autumn can be mild and dry, making it a wonderful time to be out in the garden. It's usually cooler than summer, so the job of clearing ground and digging in well-rotted compost is less taxing and rain is more likely, meaning newly planted trees and shrubs need less watering and are less likely to suffer drought-related stress. On the downside, windy weather is more prevalent, so you must have your stakes and supports ready for any new additions.

## Early autumn

Early autumn is almost the busiest harvesting time in an established fruit garden. There's plenty to pick, particularly among the tree fruit such as apples and pears, many varieties of which will be ready now. Otherwise, you can make a start on pruning cane fruit (*see* pages 69–70). Water potted plants less and stop feeding them.

Towards the end of the month remember to move tender plants, such as citrus fruit, back into the conservatory or greenhouse.

**Plant** Strawberries and most pot-grown fruit.

**Prune** Blackberries (after fruiting), boysenberries, loganberries, tayberries, tummelberries.

**Harvest** Apples, apricots, blackberries, blueberries, cherries (morello), figs (greenhouse and outdoor), filberts, grapes (indoor), greengages, melons, mulberries, passionfruit, peaches, pears (early varieties), plums, raspberries (autumn-fruiting), strawberries (perpetual-fruiting).

## Mid- to late autumn

As the weather starts to get cooler, it's a good idea to close the greenhouse early in the afternoon to trap heat, which will help to ripen indoor fruit. Set aside a day to have a clear-out and remove shading paint or blinds. Once you've harvested the last melon, dig up and discard the old plants, which will be dying by now. If you have permanent fruit growing in the greenhouse borders, work in compost or well-rotted manure around them.

Harvest grapes by cutting the stem with a pair of secateurs. Grapes don't ripen any further after picking, so pinch one off the bunch and taste it beforehand to be sure they're really ready for harvesting.

### Don't forget

Clean and sharpen all your pruning tools before and after using them, then they will be in the best condition to do a good job.

Towards the end of October, move tubs of outdoor fruit trees close to the house for protection from the worst of the wind, secure tall plants to trellis if possible or wedge them tightly together to stop them from falling over in the wind, and raise the containers up on bricks or 'pot feet' to improve drainage in wet weather.

### Climate change

For the last few years, climate change has been widely talked about in the media, by scientists and among those in government. It is almost universally accepted that the weather is not the same as it was when our grandparents were children, and it seems that overall Britain is warming up. Although we don't know for sure what the long-term effects of this will be, records show that trees are coming into leaf earlier and plants flowering sooner. While we should all try to reduce our own carbon footprint, the best thing that gardeners can do is to adapt to changing conditions, altering our habits to ensure our plants can produce the crops we plan for.

**Plant** Plant most fruit throughout the autumn season, avoiding times when the ground is unworkable due to excess wet.

**Prune** Blackberries (after fruiting).

**Harvest** Almonds, apples, citrus fruit (kumquats, lemons, limes, oranges), cobnuts, cranberries, damsons, figs (greenhouse), filberts, grapes (indoor), kiwi fruit, medlars (late October), melons, passionfruit, pears, quinces (late October), raspberries (autumn-fruiting), strawberries (perpetual-fruiting), sweet chestnuts, walnuts.

■ **Last chance to …** Always make sure you pick apples and pears before windy weather sets in. Store them carefully, discarding bruised or damaged specimens, or use them straightaway.

## The winter season

Although autumn is usually the most pleasant time to prepare and plant up a new fruit patch, early winter is often just as dry and can be quite mild. If you didn't do it earlier, get down to clearing the ground and planting new specimens. Bare-root trees can only be obtained and so planted while they are dormant, which is when they're leafless, but this is also a good time for planting pot-grown fruit (*see* pages 32–5).

In an established garden, winter is the season to prune freestanding apples and pear trees, blackcurrant bushes, and bush gooseberries and redcurrants. Prune grapevines and figs only in the very middle of winter when they are fully dormant, so they don't 'bleed'.

**Plant**  Plant most fruit during drier, milder periods. Avoid times when the soil is heavy after rain or frozen.

**Prune**  November to early or mid-March – Blackcurrants, freestanding apple and pear trees, and blueberries, medlars and quinces, if necessary.
November to end of February – Kiwi fruit and bush gooseberries,

### Heeling in bare-root plants

Bare-root plants need to be planted as soon as they arrive, otherwise they may die. If the ground is unworkable, heel them in. Dig a large hole in a sheltered spot where the ground is well drained, or in the greenhouse or polytunnel. Pile the soil you remove to one side, so the heap slopes down into the hole, then put the plant bundles with their roots in the hole and their stems lying up the slope. Cover the roots with soil. If you have nowhere else suitable, put them in a large tub and fill it with damp soil or compost.

redcurrants and whitecurrants.
December or January – All grapes (indoor and outdoor), and figs.
February – Cobnuts, filberts (late February), passionfruit, raspberries (autumn-fruiting).

**Harvest**  November – grapes (indoor), walnuts.
February to March – forced rhubarb is ready now.

Ripe walnuts will fall off the tree in their own good time. However, once a few have fallen, it pays to pick the rest, allow the shells to dry out and then store them in a cool, airy place.

■ **Take the opportunity to …**
Check all your stakes and supports as you go around pruning and tidying up. Replace any that are on their last legs and adjust ties as necessary. Freestanding trees that

have been establishing for two or three years might be able to survive without their stakes by now, but if you're in doubt, leave them in place for another year.

Build yourself a compost bin or two, if you haven't already got one (*see* page 27). Prunings from trees and bushes are rather woody. They're best shredded (*see* page 23) and even then need plenty of time to rot down. However, they're ideal for mixing with grass cuttings, which speeds up their rotting time and prevents the grass from matting into a nasty, smelly mess. Add them in layers as you add grass. If you have masses of prunings, you might also consider using them directly as a mulch after shredding (*see* page 40).

## The spring season

With the lengthening days, the weather will start to warm up and buds begin to swell and open. Many fruit plants flower before they produce leaves, so fruit gardeners love a mild, calm spring. If the weather is cold and blustery, cover blossom with horticultural fleece (*see* page 46). It might be a bit of a hassle, but it's the only way to ensure you'll get fruit. On dry, calm days get out and clear the weeds from around fruit trees, canes and bushes (*see* pages 39–40) and apply mulch. If you go to the trouble of mulching – and you should – apply it generously: 5cm (2in) around each plant is not excessive, but don't heap it up around the stems and trunks.

## Early spring

You can continue to put in new pot-grown fruit plants up to the middle or end of March. Remember to prepare the ground by forking over and removing weeds and large stones, and to add well-rotted compost to the planting hole and the soil (*see* pages 26–9). Complete any pruning before the middle of the month.

**Sow** Indoors: passionfruit.

**Plant** Strawberries and most pot-grown plants.

**Prune** Complete pruning of winter-pruned fruit (*see* page 77).

**Harvest** Forced rhubarb.

### Making leaf mould

It makes sense to collect the fallen leaves from fruit trees and shrubs and use them to make leaf mould. Quite apart from tidying up the fruit garden, it also ensures that pests and diseases are not being harboured or encouraged under the slowly rotting leaves. Make a container by wrapping plastic mesh around bamboo canes and using wire to secure it. Leaves rot down quite slowly and eventually make a soft humus that is low in nutrients but ideal for mulching.

In mid- to late spring, cover the ground where you plan to put your melons. Simple plastic sheeting will do. This will warm up the soil and ensure the melons grow away happily when you plant them out in early summer.

## Mid-spring

As their growth burgeons in mid-spring, this is the time that fruit plants begin to get really hungry. Start a regular feeding regime for plants in the fruit garden (*see* pages 38–9), as well as for pot-grown specimens. Top-dress if necessary (*see* page 34).

If you have trouble with slugs in your strawberry patch, consider using biological controls (*see* page 50). The mild, damp weather of mid- to late spring is the best time to use them and will reduce slug numbers for several weeks. The control comes as a powder and has a 'use by' date, so plan your order to coincide with suitable weather if possible.

**Sow**  Indoors: melons.

**Plant**  Blueberries, cranberries, strawberries.

**Prune**  Citrus fruit, if needed.

**Harvest**  Forced rhubarb.

■ **Last chance to …**  Pot up container-grown plants. Pot-bound plants will be starting to suffer now, and need potting on.

## Insect pests

Keep an eye on the pest situation and step in only if need be – leave nature to deal with greenfly and other insects as far as possible. You might think that the birds aren't eating them, but that's only because you aren't watching all day. Small birds such as blue tits hop around and through bushes and trees and do a very good job of clearing up unwanted aphids. If you're lucky enough to see them picking away at these pests, you will soon wish you had more insects just so they have more to eat.

Bamboo canes, hollow stems and holes drilled in wood make perfect homes for mason bees, which like to nest in narrow, tubular spaces. Other beneficial insects, including ladybirds, like similar roosts.

Forced rhubarb is tender with a wonderful delicate flavour. As long as they have a period of normal growth later, the plants don't suffer from being forced into growth early, so you can do this every year if you wish.

## Encouraging bees

In many parts of the world, bees are facing major problems, with populations much reduced and disease rife. Without bees we will not have fruit, as they're the key pollinators of our food crops. It makes sense, therefore, to encourage bees to come into your garden and, once there, to stay. The best way to do this is to plant pollen- and nectar-rich flowers and provide plenty of places for the bees to nest.

Choose a variety of flowers that bloom at different times of the year so that your bees can find sustenance all year round. Include early flowers such as forget-me-nots (*Myosotis*), aubretias and wallflowers (*Erysimum*) and late ones like ice plant (*Sedum spectabile*) and Michaelmas daisies (*Aster*). At the height of summer, there should be plenty of flowers about, but even so, you can help by choosing bee-friendly plants. These include the old-fashioned, single-flowered annuals, such as California poppy (*Eschscholzia californica*), love-in-a-mist (*Nigella*) and sunflowers (*Helianthus*), as well as perennials like fleabane (*Erigeron*), golden rod (*Solidago*) and various thistle-like plants (*Echinops*, *Eryngium*). Don't rely on more highly bred plants with double flowers, as these have less, or even no pollen or nectar, or the abundance of petals makes it difficult for the bees to reach what is there. Herbs such as borage, thyme and lavender are great choices too, as is the vegetable globe artichoke – leave one or two of the buds to open into flowers just for the bees.

You can buy nesting boxes for bumblebees, but an ordinary flowerpot or two will do the job just as well. They like to nest at ground level or underground, so dig a hole and bury each pot upside down or slightly at an angle, so the bees can use the drainage holes for access. Solitary bees make their homes in small holes in walls or in dead branches and twigs, so leave some prunings around the garden for them; alternatively, tie up small bundles of bamboo canes – cut into short lengths – for red mason bees.

## Late spring

This is a wonderful time to be in the garden, with plants growing fast and full of blossom or even beginning to develop tiny fruit. It is also a busy time for the fruit gardener, as weeds are growing fast too, and dry spells mean you must keep a close watch on newly planted fruit and any grown in pots, and water them as needed.

Continue feeding plants. Regular liquid feeds are particularly important for plants in pots, so decide on a regular day to do this and don't forget, or the plants will suffer and cropping will be reduced.

**Plant** Outside – blueberries. Under cover – melons, passionfruit.

**Prune** Snip off or 'finger-prune' fan-trained almonds, nectarines and peaches from May onwards over the summer. Prune apricots if needed.

**Harvest** Gooseberries (culinary), rhubarb.

### Greenhouses and polytunnels

As the weather warms up, greenhouses need to be shaded and damped down. Use proprietary shade paint, which you paint on outside and wash off in the autumn, or blinds. There are various types of blind available: they're not cheap, but they are more convenient than paint, since you have the option to adjust them on cloudier days. Water all surfaces on hot days to keep the atmosphere damp, and open doors and vents; automatic vents come in handy at this time of the year because they do this job for you.

The plastic used to cover polytunnels is not fully transparent, so shading isn't a problem; however, you must open the ends for ventilation. Condensation forms on the inside of the plastic, which helps with damping down, although during really dry spells, it doesn't hurt to water inside too.

Culinary gooseberries can be picked from late spring. They're hard and much too sour to eat raw, but they're perfect for stewing with a little sugar and for putting in cooked desserts such as gooseberry pies and fools.

### Don't forget

Plants are growing very fast at this time of the year, so it pays to make a habit of checking your plant ties on a regular basis and adding more as necessary. You could do it at the same time as pruning.

## The summer season

Summer is a time of anticipation in the fruit garden, as all sorts of fruits are just starting to ripen and the rest will soon follow suit. If you're growing trained (supported) fruit trees, summer is a busy time: they all need careful pruning to keep their productivity high. Otherwise, as long as you've got on top of the weeding and have established a regular feeding regime, you can relax and look forward to feasting on the fruits of your labours.

If you're an energetic gardener, you might like to start improvements to your fruit garden – supports could be replaced (or removed in the case of more mature freestanding trees), arches, trellises and fruit cages could be planned and additional planting could be considered.

## Early summer

Water is vital for a healthy, juicy crop, so remember to water well and regularly during dry spells. Fruit under cover will need much more water now and, outdoors, strawberries are particularly vulnerable to dry weather as they have shallow roots. Fruit bushes and vines also need plenty of water, and in summer containers more or less rely on you for their water. Even if it rains, check pots daily.

Move citrus plants out of the conservatory now, and onto a sheltered patio. Net strawberries to protect the growing fruit from birds (*see* pages 46–7), and continue to weed and hoe as necessary.

**Plant**  Melons (outside and under cover), passionfruit.

Thinning developing apples is a sensible measure in early summer. You won't necessarily get more fruit if you leave them all on, and thinning should ensure that the apples you do get will be bigger and tastier.

**Prune**  Fan-trained almonds, nectarines and peaches, using your fingers to pinch off unwanted growth throughout summer; figs.

**Harvest**  Gooseberries (culinary), raspberries (late June), redcurrants, rhubarb, strawberries, whitecurrants.

■ **Take the opportunity to …**
Check out your storage facilities for apples, pears, nuts and so on later in the year. Clear out a corner of the shed or garage and get hold of some shelving or consider making some racks so you are ready when the time comes.

Ripe raspberries are very soft and easily bruised, but this is the moment when they're best eaten. Pick only what you need, putting them carefully into a wide-based container in shallow layers.

## Gardening clubs and shows

Most gardeners are friendly folk and very happy to share their knowledge, and they often do this via gardening clubs. These are usually informal and offer the opportunity for plant swaps as well as a social occasion. Many villages and towns have a gardening club (look in parish magazines or on noticeboards), and most also have a summer flower and produce show. If you're particularly proud of your crops, it can be fun to enter some classes. Although these shows are generally well supported, it's often the same people who have the job of organizing them year after year, and the same ones who enter the classes too, so new faces will be welcomed, especially if you volunteer to help in some way. Even if you don't win any prizes, you'll meet plenty of like-minded people and learn lots along the way.

## Midsummer

This is the peak time for soft fruit production. You'll be busy picking ripe crops and netting ripening ones. Start picking early apple varieties; harvest as you need them and eat them straight from the tree.

Again, continue to pay great attention to watering, increasing the amounts or times to ensure pot-grown fruit and those under cover never go dry. With increased water goes an increased need for liquid feeds.

Summer-prune trained fruit trees and bushes in late July or early August. Pinch out the growing tips of melons once four fruit are set.

**Prune** Trained trees, such as almonds, apples, apricots, cherries, mulberries, peaches and nectarines, pears and plums; grapes (indoor and outdoor, depending on your growing method); gooseberries, kiwis, redcurrants and whitecurrants.

**Harvest** Apples (early varieties), apricots, blackberries (early varieties), blackcurrants, blueberries, boysenberries, cherries, citrus fruit (lemons, limes, kumquats, oranges), figs (greenhouse), gooseberries (dessert), loganberries, peaches, plums, raspberries (summer-fruiting), redcurrants, rhubarb, strawberries (summer and perpetual- fruiting varieties), tayberries, tummelberries, whitecurrants.

■ **Last chance to ...** Propagate strawberries from runners (see page 115). Wait until you've harvested all the fruit and then choose some healthy plantlets to replace your older plants.

Blackcurrants can be a bit of a fiddle to pick, as they're easily squashed in the process. It's often easier to snip off whole 'strigs' and separate off the individual berries back in the kitchen.

## Late summer

In a dry summer, watering might well have become a bit of a chore by now, but it's really vital that you continue your watering regime throughout the season. If you're going away on holiday, arrange for a friend or neighbour to drop in regularly and take over this job for you. As an incentive (and to avoid waste), tell them to help themselves to any fruit that's ready while you're away. Feeding, weeding and picking are also regular jobs at this time of the year.

**Plant** Strawberries.

**Prune** Raspberries (summer-fruiting varieties after fruiting); continue to 'finger-prune' fan-trained trees, such as almonds, peaches and nectarines.

**Harvest** Apples (early varieties), apricots, blackberries, blackcurrants, blueberries, boysenberries, cherries (morello and other varieties), citrus fruit (lemons, kumquats, oranges, limes), figs (greenhouse and outdoor), greengages, loganberries, melons, mulberries, nectarines, passionfruit, peaches, plums, raspberries (autumn-fruiting), redcurrants, strawberries (perpetual-fruiting), tayberries, tummelberries, whitecurrants.

■ **After your holiday ...** Use some of that post-holiday enthusiasm to start planning for the following year. Take a critical look at the fruit garden and decide where you think improvements could be made – making changes is all part of the fun of gardening.

# Index

Page numbers in *italics* refer to plants illustrated and/or described in the A–Z of fruit.

# Acknowledgements

**BBC Books and OutHouse** would like to thank the following for their assistance in preparing this book: Candida Frith-MacDonald for help with illustrations; Phil McCann for advice and guidance; Joanne Forrest Smith for picture research; Lindsey Brown for proofreading; June Wilkins for the index.

## Picture credits
**Key**  t = top, b = bottom, l = left, r = right, c = centre

**All photos by Jonathan Buckley** except the following:

**GAP Photos** Lee Avison 87tr; Pernilla Bergdahl 8; Dave Bevan 83b & t; Christina Bollen 117; Mark Bolton 105bl; Elke Borkowski 24, 95, 119; Leigh Clapp, Location: Bardsey 38; FhF Greenmedia 77bc, 108b; Victoria Firmston 88t; Tim Gainey 2–3; John Glover 15tr, 77bl, 82, 85, 86, 93b, 102, 104tl; Neil Holmes 4–5, 20tc, 104tr; Martin Hughes-Jones 68; Dianna Jazwinski 20trb; Janet Johnson 92; Andrea Jones 88b, 116, 118; Michael Howes 93t; Michael King 48t; Zara Napier 72; Clive Nichols 5r; S&O 10, 103; J S Sira 36; Friedrich Strauss 15tc, 21t, 35, 96; Graham Strong 84; Maddie Thornhill 91, 109br; Juliette Wade 121t; Rachel Warne 9; Jo Whitworth 11t, 97; Rob Whitworth 101; Visions 100bl

**Garden World Images** L Thomas 87tc

**iStockphoto.com** 79, 98, 99

**Robin Whitecross** 17tr, 47(1 & 2), 55b

**Thanks are also due to** the following designers and owners whose gardens appear in the book:

Terence Conran, RHS Chelsea Flower Show 1999 16l; Patricia Fox, RHS Chelsea Flower Show 2009 20b; Alan Gray and Graham Robeson, East Ruston Old Vicarage, Norfolk 50; Bunny Guinness 104tl; Simon Hopkinson, Hollington Nurseries, Buckinghamshire 16r; Fiona Lawrenson 15tr; Christopher Lloyd, Great Dixter, East Sussex 11b, 23, 49, 65; Mr and Mrs Mogford 21l, 31; Sarah Raven, Perch Hill, East Sussex 21r, 47tr

While every effort has been made to trace and acknowledge all copyright holders, the publisher would like to apologize should there be any errors or omissions.